Discover Virgin Islands

AVERY B. HODGES

Published by AVERY B. HODGES, 2023.

DISCOVER VIRGIN ISLANDS

First edition. October 6, 2023.

ISBN: 979-8223794240

Written by AVERY B. HODGES.

Table of Contents

Chapter 1: Introduction to United States Virgin Islands

Welcome to the enchanting United States Virgin Islands, a tropical paradise nestled in the Caribbean Sea. This chapter serves as a gateway to understanding the captivating blend of geography, history, culture, and attractions that make these islands a truly unique destination for travelers seeking an unforgettable experience.

1.1 Geography

The United States Virgin Islands, also known as USVI, is an archipelago consisting of three main islands: St. Thomas, St. John, and St. Croix. These islands, along with several smaller ones, are located in the northeastern Caribbean Sea, east of Puerto Rico. The USVI is an unincorporated territory of the United States, offering visitors a seamless blend of American comforts and Caribbean charm.

1.2 History

The rich history of the United States Virgin Islands dates back thousands of years. Originally inhabited by the Ciboney, Arawak, and Carib indigenous peoples, the islands were later explored by Christopher Columbus during his second voyage in 1493. Over the centuries, the islands were colonized by various European powers, including the Spanish, Dutch, English, French, and Danish. In 1917, the United States purchased the islands from Denmark, establishing its current territorial status.

1.3 Culture

The cultural tapestry of the United States Virgin Islands is a vibrant fusion of African, European, and Caribbean influences. The locals, known as Virgin Islanders, warmly embrace their diverse heritage, which is reflected in their cuisine, music, dance, and art. Experience the lively rhythms of calypso, reggae, and steel pan music, indulge in mouthwatering local delicacies like conch fritters and johnnycakes, and explore the colorful local crafts and artwork that showcase the islands' unique identity.

1.4 Attractions

The United States Virgin Islands offer an abundance of attractions for every type of traveler. From pristine white sandy beaches and crystal-clear turquoise waters to lush tropical rainforests and historic landmarks, there is something for everyone to enjoy. Explore the vibrant coral reefs while snorkeling or diving, hike through the picturesque national parks, visit historic sites like Fort Christiansvaern on St. Croix or Blackbeard's Castle on St. Thomas, or simply relax and soak up the sun on one of the many idyllic beaches.

Whether you seek adventure, relaxation, or cultural immersion, the United States Virgin Islands has it all. From its breathtaking natural beauty to its rich history and vibrant culture, this tropical paradise promises an unforgettable experience for those who venture to its shores. So, pack your bags, leave your worries behind, and get ready to embark on an extraordinary journey through the United States Virgin Islands.

Chapter 2: When to Visit United States Virgin Islands

The United States Virgin Islands, an enchanting Caribbean destination, offer a year-round tropical paradise for visitors. However, certain times of the year may be more suitable depending on your preferences and interests. In this chapter, we will provide valuable tips for planning when to go on your tourist trip to the United States Virgin Islands.

1. Peak Season: December to April

If you prefer vibrant festivals, bustling crowds, and ideal weather conditions, then the peak season from December to April is the perfect time to visit the United States Virgin Islands. During this period, the islands experience pleasant temperatures ranging from 75°F to 85°F (24°C to 29°C), making it an ideal escape from colder climates. However, it's important to note that prices for accommodation and activities tend to be higher during this time, and popular attractions may be crowded.

2. Shoulder Season: May to August

The shoulder season, from May to August, offers a great balance between favorable weather and affordability. Temperatures range from 80°F to 90°F (27°C to 32°C), providing ample opportunity for sunbathing, swimming, and engaging in water sports. This period also sees fewer tourists, allowing you to explore the islands at a more relaxed pace. It's worth noting that occasional rain showers may occur during this time, but they are usually short-lived.

3. Off-Peak Season: September to November

For those seeking a quieter and more budget-friendly experience, the off-peak season from September to November is an excellent choice. While temperatures remain warm, ranging from 75°F to 85°F (24°C to 29°C), this period coincides with the Atlantic hurricane season. While the chances of encountering a hurricane are low, it's important to stay updated on weather forecasts and consider travel insurance. Despite the slight risk, visiting during this time allows you to enjoy discounted rates on accommodations and activities, as well as fewer tourists.

4. Special Events and Festivals

If you have a particular interest in local culture and vibrant celebrations, consider planning your visit around the various events and festivals that take place throughout the year. The United States Virgin Islands host a range of exciting festivities, such as the St. Thomas Carnival in April, the St. John Festival in June, and the Crucian Christmas Festival in December. These events provide a unique opportunity to immerse yourself in the local traditions, music, and cuisine.

5. Nature and Wildlife Enthusiasts

If you are an avid nature lover, consider visiting the United States Virgin Islands during the months of February to April. This period is ideal for birdwatching, as migratory birds make their way through the islands. Additionally, humpback whales can often be spotted off the coast of St. Croix during their annual migration from January to March.

By considering your preferences, budget, and desired experiences, you can choose the perfect time to visit the United States Virgin Islands. Whether you opt for the peak, shoulder, or off-peak season, this tropical paradise promises an unforgettable vacation filled with stunning beaches, crystal-clear waters, and rich cultural heritage.

Chapter 3: What to Pack for Your Trip to the United States Virgin Islands

Introduction:

Preparing for a trip to the United States Virgin Islands requires careful consideration of what to pack. The tropical climate and breathtaking landscapes of these islands make it essential to pack wisely. In this chapter, we will guide you through the essentials and provide helpful tips to ensure you have a memorable and comfortable vacation.

1. Clothing:

The United States Virgin Islands boast warm temperatures year-round, so packing lightweight and breathable clothing is essential. Here are some recommendations:

- Lightweight, loose-fitting shirts and blouses
- Shorts and skirts made of breathable fabrics
- Swimwear for beach excursions
- Comfortable walking shoes or sandals
- A light jacket or sweater for cooler evenings
- Don't forget a hat, sunglasses, and sunscreen to protect yourself from the sun's rays.

2. Outdoor Essentials:

Exploring the United States Virgin Islands means immersing yourself in nature's beauty. To make the most of your outdoor adventures, consider packing the following:

- A sturdy backpack for day trips
- A reusable water bottle to stay hydrated
- Insect repellent to ward off bugs
- Snorkeling gear for underwater exploration
- A beach towel and beach mat for lounging by the sea
- A waterproof bag to protect your belongings during water activities

3. Electronics and Miscellaneous Items:

While it's essential to disconnect and enjoy the natural wonders of the islands, some electronics and miscellaneous items can enhance your experience. Consider packing the following:

- A camera or smartphone with a good camera to capture stunning moments
- Adapters and chargers for your electronic devices
- A power bank to ensure your devices stay charged on the go
- A small first aid kit with basic medical supplies
- Travel-sized toiletries and personal hygiene products
- Any necessary prescription medications

4. Travel Documents:

To ensure a smooth and stress-free trip, don't forget to pack all the necessary travel documents. These may include:

- A valid passport for international travelers
- A driver's license or identification card
- Printed copies of your hotel reservations and flight itineraries
- Travel insurance documents, if applicable
- Credit cards and some cash for emergencies or small purchases

Conclusion:

Packing for your trip to the United States Virgin Islands requires careful consideration of the climate, activities, and your personal needs. By following the recommendations in this chapter, you can ensure a comfortable and enjoyable vacation. Remember to pack light, prioritize essentials, and leave some room for souvenirs to commemorate your unforgettable experiences in this tropical paradise.

Chapter 4: Geography and Climate of United States Virgin Islands

Introduction:

Welcome to Chapter 4 of our tourist guide on the United States Virgin Islands. In this chapter, we will explore the captivating geography and climate of these beautiful islands. From majestic mountains to pristine coastlines, the United States Virgin Islands offer a unique blend of natural wonders and tropical paradise. Join us as we delve into the physical features and climatic conditions that make these islands a true haven for visitors from around the world.

Geography of United States Virgin Islands:

The United States Virgin Islands are located in the Caribbean Sea, east of Puerto Rico. Comprised of three main islands – St. Croix, St. John, and St. Thomas – this archipelago boasts a diverse range of landscapes. Let's take a closer look at the physical geography of each island.

1. St. Croix:

St. Croix, the largest of the three islands, is known for its rolling hills and fertile plains. The eastern part of the island is characterized by lush vegetation and tropical rainforests, while the western side features a more arid climate and cactus-studded landscapes. The island's southern coast is adorned with stunning white-sand beaches, offering visitors a tranquil escape.

2. St. John:

St. John, the smallest of the three islands, is a true gem of natural beauty. Two-thirds of the island is protected as part of the Virgin Islands National Park, ensuring its pristine state. St. John is renowned for its untouched beaches, crystal-clear waters, and vibrant coral reefs. Hiking enthusiasts can explore the island's lush forests, which are home to diverse flora and fauna.

3. St. Thomas:

St. Thomas, the most developed of the three islands, is a bustling hub for tourism and commerce. Its mountainous terrain provides visitors with breathtaking panoramic views of the Caribbean Sea. The island boasts stunning beaches, including the famous Magens Bay, which has been consistently ranked among the world's most beautiful beaches. St. Thomas also offers a vibrant nightlife and a wide range of shopping opportunities.

Climate of United States Virgin Islands:

The United States Virgin Islands experience a tropical climate, characterized by warm temperatures and high humidity throughout the year. The islands enjoy a pleasant average temperature of around 80°F (27°C), making it an ideal destination for sun-seekers. However, it is essential to be prepared for occasional rainfall, as the islands receive most of their precipitation during the wet season, which typically runs from May to November.

During the wet season, visitors can expect brief and intense showers, often followed by clear skies. These rain showers contribute to the lush greenery and vibrant flora that grace the islands. The dry season, from December to April, offers visitors more consistent sunshine and lower chances of rain.

It is important to note that the United States Virgin Islands are susceptible to tropical storms and hurricanes, particularly during the Atlantic hurricane season, which spans from June to November. Visitors are advised to stay informed about weather conditions and follow any instructions or warnings issued by local authorities.

Conclusion:

As we conclude this chapter on the geography and climate of the United States Virgin Islands, we hope you have gained a deeper understanding of the natural wonders that await you on these enchanting islands. From the diverse landscapes of St. Croix to the untouched beauty of St. John and the vibrant atmosphere of St. Thomas, each island offers a unique experience for every visitor. Embrace the tropical climate, enjoy the breathtaking views, and immerse yourself in the natural splendor of the United States Virgin Islands.

Chapter 5: The Regions of United States Virgin Islands

Introduction:

Welcome to the United States Virgin Islands, a tropical paradise located in the Caribbean Sea. This chapter will take you on a journey through the different regions of this breathtaking destination, each with its own unique characteristics and attractions. From the vibrant culture of St. Thomas to the untouched beauty of St. John and the historical charm of St. Croix, there is something here for every type of traveler. So, pack your bags and get ready to explore the regions of the United States Virgin Islands!

1. St. Thomas - The Vibrant Hub:

St. Thomas, the most cosmopolitan of the three main islands, is known for its vibrant atmosphere and bustling towns. Start your journey in Charlotte Amalie, the capital city, where you can explore the historic district filled with Danish colonial architecture. Don't miss a visit to Blackbeard's Castle, a legendary pirate lookout offering panoramic views of the island. St. Thomas is also renowned for its duty-free shopping, with countless boutiques and jewelry stores offering tax-free luxury goods. For beach lovers, Magens Bay, one of the world's most beautiful beaches, is a must-visit spot.

2. St. John - The Untouched Gem:

Just a short ferry ride from St. Thomas lies the tranquil island of St. John. With two-thirds of its land designated as a national park, St. John is a nature lover's paradise. Hiking enthusiasts can explore the various trails, such as the Reef Bay Trail, which leads to ancient petroglyphs and a stunning waterfall. Snorkelers and divers will be captivated by the pristine coral reefs surrounding the island, teeming with colorful marine life. Trunk Bay, with its crystal-clear waters and underwater snorkeling trail, is often ranked among the world's top beaches.

3. St. Croix - The Historical Gem:

St. Croix, the largest of the three main islands, is rich in history and culture. Start your exploration in Christiansted, the island's charming main town, where you can wander through the cobblestone streets lined with colorful Danish colonial buildings. Visit the imposing Fort Christiansvaern, a UNESCO World Heritage site, and learn about the island's colonial past. St. Croix is also known for its vibrant culinary scene, with a fusion of Caribbean and European flavors. Don't miss a taste of the local favorite, Cruzan Rum, at the Cruzan Rum Distillery.

4. Water Island - The Hidden Paradise:

Tucked away just off the coast of St. Thomas, Water Island is a hidden gem waiting to be discovered. With a population of fewer than 200 people, this tiny island offers a peaceful and secluded escape from the bustling tourist spots. Spend your days lounging on Honeymoon Beach, a pristine stretch of white sand, or explore the underwater wonders while snorkeling in the turquoise waters. For a unique experience, visit the historic Fort Segarra, which offers panoramic views of the surrounding islands.

Conclusion:

The United States Virgin Islands is a destination that truly has it all. From the vibrant energy of St. Thomas to the untouched beauty of St. John and the historical charm of St. Croix, each region offers a unique experience for every traveler. Whether you're seeking adventure, relaxation, or a cultural immersion, the United States Virgin Islands will leave you with memories to last a lifetime. So, come and discover the magic of these incredible islands and let the beauty of the Caribbean captivate your senses.

Chapter 6: A Tapestry of History and Culture in the United States Virgin Islands

Introduction:

The United States Virgin Islands, an enchanting archipelago in the Caribbean Sea, holds a rich tapestry of history and culture. From its earliest inhabitants to the present day, this chapter will provide a brief overview of the captivating past that has shaped the vibrant present of these islands. We will explore key historical events, influential figures, and significant sites that continue to leave an indelible mark on the United States Virgin Islands.

Section 1: The Indigenous People:

The United States Virgin Islands were once inhabited by the indigenous Taíno people. These resourceful and skilled individuals lived harmoniously with the land, leaving behind remnants of their culture, such as petroglyphs and artifacts. We will delve into their way of life, customs, and the impact they had on the islands' early development.

Section 2: European Exploration and Colonization:

The arrival of European explorers brought significant changes to the United States Virgin Islands. We will explore the encounters between Christopher Columbus, Sir Francis Drake, and other explorers, as well as the subsequent colonization efforts by the Dutch, Danish, French, and British. The struggles for control over these islands will be examined, shedding light on the diverse cultural influences that exist today.

Section 3: The Danish Era:

The Danish West India Company established a strong presence in the United States Virgin Islands during the 17th and 18th centuries. We will delve into the impact of the Danish colonial rule, including the establishment of plantations, the transatlantic slave trade, and the rise of the sugar industry. Key historical figures, such as Governor Peter von Scholten, will be highlighted for their contributions to the islands' history.

Section 4: The Transfer of Ownership:

In 1917, the United States purchased the Virgin Islands from Denmark, forever changing the course of history for the archipelago. We will explore the reasons behind this acquisition and the subsequent impact it had on the islands' culture, economy, and governance. The process of assimilation and the struggles faced by the local population will also be examined.

Section 5: Cultural Fusion:

The United States Virgin Islands is a melting pot of cultures, resulting from its diverse history. We will explore the fusion of African, European, and Caribbean influences that have shaped the islands' unique cultural identity. From music and dance, such as the vibrant sounds of calypso and reggae, to the mouthwatering culinary delights, the chapter will highlight the cultural tapestry that makes this destination truly one-of-a-kind.

Section 6: Historical Sites and Landmarks:

This section will showcase the historical sites and landmarks that serve as a testament to the United States Virgin Islands' captivating past. From the imposing Fort Christian in Charlotte Amalie to the haunting ruins of plantation estates, we will guide you through these significant locations, providing insight into their historical significance and cultural importance.

Conclusion:

As we conclude this chapter on the history and culture of the United States Virgin Islands, we hope to have provided a glimpse into the captivating past that has shaped this enchanting archipelago. From the indigenous Taíno people to the influences of European colonization and the fusion of diverse cultures, the United States

Virgin Islands stand as a testament to the resilience and vibrancy of its people. By understanding and appreciating this rich history, visitors can truly immerse themselves in the cultural tapestry that makes these islands a captivating destination.

Chapter 7: Language and People of United States Virgin Islands

Introduction:

The United States Virgin Islands, located in the Caribbean, is a captivating destination known for its stunning beaches, vibrant culture, and warm hospitality. As a traveler, understanding the languages spoken and the social customs and etiquette of the locals can greatly enhance your experience. In this chapter, we will provide a brief overview of the languages spoken in the US Virgin Islands, along with some common phrases, language tips for travelers, and insights into the social customs and etiquette of the local people.

Languages Spoken:

English is the official language of the United States Virgin Islands. Being a US territory, English is widely spoken and understood across the islands. However, due to the cultural diversity and historical influences, you may also encounter locals speaking other languages such as Spanish, French, and Creole. These languages are often used within specific communities or households, adding to the rich linguistic tapestry of the islands.

Common Phrases:

While English is the primary language, learning a few common phrases in the local dialect can help you connect with the people and show your appreciation for their culture. Here are some phrases that will come in handy:

1. Good morning/afternoon/evening - Good mahnin/afternoon/evenin
2. Thank you - Tank yuh
3. How are you? - How yuh doin'?
4. Where is...? - Wha' deh...?
5. Can you help me? - Can yuh help me?

6. I would like... - Ah wah...

7. Cheers! - Bless up!

Language Tips for Travelers:

1. English proficiency: As English is widely spoken, you will have no trouble communicating with locals, especially in tourist areas. However, it is always helpful to speak slowly and clearly, especially if you encounter someone with limited English proficiency.

2. Embrace the local dialect: While English is the main language, you may notice a distinctive local dialect known as Virgin Islands Creole English. Embrace the unique expressions and phrases you come across, and don't hesitate to ask for clarification if needed.

Social Customs and Etiquette:

The people of the United States Virgin Islands are known for their warm and friendly nature. Understanding and respecting their social customs and etiquette will help you connect with the locals on a deeper level. Here are some key points to keep in mind:

1. Greetings: When meeting someone, a warm smile and a friendly greeting are customary. Handshakes are the most common form of greeting, although close friends and family may exchange hugs or kisses on the cheek.

2. Punctuality: While being on time is generally appreciated, the concept of island time is prevalent in the US Virgin Islands. Don't be surprised if meetings or events start a little later than scheduled – it's all part of the relaxed island lifestyle.

3. Respect for elders: The local culture places great emphasis on respecting elders. It is customary to address older individuals with titles such as Mr. or Ms. followed by their last name, unless they specify otherwise.

4. Dress code: The US Virgin Islands have a casual dress code due to the tropical climate. Light and comfortable clothing, such as shorts, t-shirts, and sundresses, are suitable for most occasions. However, it is

advisable to dress more conservatively when visiting religious sites or attending formal events.

Conclusion:

Understanding the languages spoken, learning a few common phrases, and respecting the social customs and etiquette of the United States Virgin Islands will undoubtedly enrich your travel experience. By embracing the local culture and connecting with the friendly locals, you will create lasting memories and forge meaningful connections during your visit to this captivating Caribbean destination.

Chapter 8: Traditional Cuisine of the United States Virgin Islands

Introduction:

The United States Virgin Islands is not only known for its stunning beaches and vibrant culture but also for its rich and diverse culinary traditions. Influenced by African, European, and Caribbean flavors, the traditional cuisine of the US Virgin Islands offers a unique gastronomic experience. In this chapter, we will delve into the most popular dishes and ingredients, guide you to the best places to savor authentic local food, and even provide you with some cooking tips and recipes to recreate these flavors in your own kitchen.

1. A Fusion of Flavors:

The traditional cuisine of the US Virgin Islands is a delightful blend of African, European, and Caribbean influences. The African heritage is reflected in the use of spices and cooking techniques, while the European influence can be seen in the incorporation of ingredients like pork, beef, and fish. Caribbean flavors, on the other hand, bring a tropical twist with the use of fruits, vegetables, and exotic spices.

2. Must-Try Dishes:

a) Callaloo Soup: A hearty and nutritious soup made with leafy greens, okra, crab, and sometimes even coconut milk. This dish perfectly showcases the African and Caribbean fusion flavors of the islands.

b) Johnny Cake: A traditional cornmeal flatbread that is often served as a side dish or as a breakfast staple. Enjoy it with butter or honey for a truly authentic taste.

c) Saltfish and Dumplings: A classic dish made with salted codfish and dumplings, usually served with a side of boiled root vegetables. This dish represents the European influence on the islands' cuisine.

d) Conch Fritters: A popular appetizer made from conch meat mixed with flour, vegetables, and spices, then deep-fried to perfection. These fritters are a true taste of the Caribbean.

e) Pate: A savory pastry filled with various fillings such as chicken, beef, or vegetables. This handheld delight is perfect for a quick snack or on-the-go meal.

3. Where to Find the Best Food:

To truly experience the traditional cuisine of the US Virgin Islands, venture beyond the tourist areas and explore the local food scene. Visit local eateries, known as food shacks where you can savor authentic dishes prepared by talented home cooks. Some popular spots to try include:

- Glady's Café: Located in St. Thomas, this charming café offers a variety of local dishes, including Callaloo Soup and Saltfish and Dumplings.

- Nancy's Restaurant: Situated in St. Croix, Nancy's is renowned for its delectable Conch Fritters and other seafood specialties.

- Cuzzin's Caribbean Restaurant and Bar: Found in St. John, this restaurant serves up mouthwatering Pates and other traditional island favorites.

4. Cooking Tips and Recipes:

For those who want to bring the flavors of the US Virgin Islands into their own kitchen, here are a couple of cooking tips and recipes to get you started:

a) When cooking traditional dishes, don't be afraid to experiment with spices and seasonings. Use ingredients like thyme, allspice, and Scotch bonnet peppers to add depth and heat to your dishes.

b) Recipe: Callaloo Soup

Ingredients:

- 2 cups fresh callaloo leaves (substitute spinach if unavailable)

- 1 cup crab meat

- 1 onion, chopped

- 2 cloves garlic, minced
- 1 cup coconut milk
- Salt and pepper to taste

Instructions:

1. In a large pot, sauté the onions and garlic until translucent.
2. Add the callaloo leaves and cook until wilted.
3. Stir in the crab meat and coconut milk.
4. Season with salt and pepper to taste.
5. Simmer for 15-20 minutes, allowing the flavors to meld together.
6. Serve hot and enjoy the taste of the islands!

Conclusion:

The traditional cuisine of the United States Virgin Islands is a true reflection of the islands' cultural diversity and history. From savory soups to delectable pastries, the flavors of the US Virgin Islands are sure to tantalize your taste buds. By exploring local eateries and trying your hand at traditional recipes, you can fully immerse yourself in the culinary delights of this tropical paradise.

Chapter 9: Modern Cuisine of the United States Virgin Islands

Introduction:

The United States Virgin Islands is not only known for its pristine beaches and stunning landscapes but also for its vibrant and diverse culinary scene. Influenced by African, European, and Caribbean flavors, the modern cuisine of the US Virgin Islands offers a unique fusion of tastes and ingredients. In this chapter, we will explore the most popular dishes and ingredients, reveal where to find the best food in the country, and even provide some cooking tips and recipes for you to try at home.

1. A Fusion of Flavors:

The modern cuisine of the United States Virgin Islands is a true reflection of the islands' rich history and cultural diversity. African, European, and Caribbean influences have blended together to create a unique culinary experience. From spicy jerk chicken to flavorful seafood dishes, the local cuisine is a celebration of bold and vibrant flavors.

2. Must-Try Dishes:

When visiting the US Virgin Islands, there are several dishes that should not be missed. One such dish is the traditional Johnny Cake a delicious fried bread made from cornmeal or flour. Another local favorite is Kallaloo a hearty soup made with leafy greens, okra, and various meats or seafood. For seafood lovers, Conch Fritters are a must-try. These crispy fritters made from conch meat are a popular appetizer across the islands.

3. Fresh and Local Ingredients:

The abundance of fresh and local ingredients is one of the highlights of the modern cuisine in the US Virgin Islands. With its tropical climate and fertile soil, the islands offer a wide variety of fruits and vegetables. From juicy mangoes and papayas to flavorful guavas and passion fruits, the local produce adds a burst of freshness to every dish. Seafood, including fish, lobster, and conch, is also a staple in the islands' cuisine.

4. Where to Find the Best Food:

To truly experience the modern cuisine of the US Virgin Islands, you must explore the local food scene. St. Thomas, St. Croix, and St. John offer a plethora of dining options, ranging from casual beachfront eateries to upscale restaurants. In Charlotte Amalie, the capital of the islands, you can find a wide range of international cuisines, including Italian, French, and Asian. For an authentic taste of the local cuisine, head to the local food trucks and street vendors, where you can savor delicious dishes at affordable prices.

5. Cooking Tips and Recipes:

If you're feeling inspired to recreate the flavors of the US Virgin Islands in your own kitchen, we've got you covered. Here are a few cooking tips to help you along the way:

- Experiment with local spices: The islands are known for their flavorful spices, such as allspice, nutmeg, and Scotch bonnet peppers. Don't be afraid to add a pinch of these spices to elevate your dishes.

- Embrace the seafood: Incorporate fresh seafood, such as snapper or mahi-mahi, into your recipes. Grilling or pan-searing fish with a squeeze of lime juice can create a mouthwatering dish.

- Get creative with tropical fruits: Incorporate tropical fruits like mangoes, pineapples, and bananas into your desserts or salads for a burst of sweetness and freshness.

To get you started, here's a recipe for a classic Virgin Islands dish:

Recipe: Rum Cake

Ingredients:

- 2 cups all-purpose flour
- 1 ½ cups granulated sugar
- 1 cup unsalted butter, softened

- 4 eggs
- 1 cup milk
- 1 teaspoon vanilla extract
- ½ cup dark rum
- 1 teaspoon baking powder
- Pinch of salt

Instructions:

1. Preheat the oven to 350°F (175°C). Grease and flour a Bundt pan.

2. In a large mixing bowl, cream together the butter and sugar until light and fluffy.

3. Beat in the eggs, one at a time, followed by the vanilla extract and rum.

4. In a separate bowl, whisk together the flour, baking powder, and salt. Gradually add the dry ingredients to the butter mixture, alternating with the milk.

5. Pour the batter into the prepared Bundt pan and smooth the top.

6. Bake for approximately 45-50 minutes or until a toothpick inserted into the center comes out clean.

7. Allow the cake to cool in the pan for 10 minutes before transferring it to a wire rack to cool completely.

8. Optional: Drizzle a rum glaze over the cooled cake for an extra kick of flavor.

9. Serve and enjoy!

Conclusion:

The modern cuisine of the United States Virgin Islands is a delightful fusion of flavors, influenced by the islands' diverse cultural heritage. From traditional dishes to innovative creations, the local cuisine offers a feast for the senses. Whether you're exploring the local food scene or trying your hand at cooking the recipes at home, the flavors of the US Virgin Islands are sure to leave a lasting impression.

Chapter 10: Drinks and Beverages of the United States Virgin Islands

Introduction:

The United States Virgin Islands is not only known for its stunning beaches and vibrant culture but also for its unique and refreshing drinks and beverages. From tropical cocktails to local brews, the islands offer a wide variety of options for both alcoholic and non-alcoholic beverage enthusiasts. In this chapter, we will explore the most popular drinks and where to find the best spots to quench your thirst in the United States Virgin Islands.

1. The Famous Bushwacker:

One cannot talk about drinks in the Virgin Islands without mentioning the famous Bushwacker. This creamy and indulgent cocktail is a favorite among locals and tourists alike. Made with rum, Kahlua, Baileys, Amaretto, coconut cream, and chocolate syrup, the Bushwacker is the perfect treat to cool down under the Caribbean sun. You can find this delightful concoction at beach bars, such as The Beach Bar on St. John or Duffy's Love Shack on St. Thomas.

2. Cruzan Rum:

The United States Virgin Islands is home to the world-renowned Cruzan Rum Distillery, which has been producing high-quality rum since 1760. A visit to the distillery on St. Croix is a must for rum enthusiasts. Take a tour and learn about the rum-making process, from the sugarcane fields to the aging barrels. Don't forget to sample the different flavors of Cruzan Rum, including their popular dark and flavored rums.

3. Local Craft Beers:

For beer lovers, the United States Virgin Islands offers a growing craft beer scene. St. John Brewers on St. John Island is a local brewery known for their handcrafted beers made with Caribbean ingredients.

From their Tropical Mango Pale Ale to their Island Hoppin' IPA, you can enjoy unique flavors that reflect the spirit of the islands. Other notable breweries include Leatherback Brewing Company on St. Croix and Brewer's Bay Beach Bar on Tortola.

4. Fresh Fruit Juices:

If you prefer non-alcoholic options, the United States Virgin Islands has an abundance of fresh fruit juices to quench your thirst. Try the local favorite, soursop juice, made from the tropical fruit known for its creamy texture and sweet-sour flavor. Other popular choices include passionfruit juice, guava juice, and mango juice. You can find these refreshing beverages at local fruit stands, juice bars, and even some restaurants.

5. Virgin Island Coffee:

Coffee lovers will be delighted to know that the United States Virgin Islands also offers its own unique blend of coffee. Grown in the fertile volcanic soil of St. Thomas, Virgin Island Coffee is known for its rich and smooth flavor. Visit local coffee shops like Barefoot Buddha or Virgin Islands Coffee Roasters to savor a cup of freshly brewed coffee while enjoying the island's laid-back atmosphere.

Conclusion:

The United States Virgin Islands is not only a paradise for beach lovers but also for those who appreciate a good drink. From the famous Bushwacker cocktail to locally brewed craft beers and fresh fruit juices, there is something to satisfy every palate. Whether you're lounging on the beach or exploring the islands, be sure to indulge in the unique and refreshing drinks and beverages that the United States Virgin Islands has to offer.

Chapter 11: Dining out in the United States Virgin Islands

Introduction:

The United States Virgin Islands offer a delightful fusion of Caribbean flavors, making it a paradise for food enthusiasts. From casual beachside eateries to upscale fine dining establishments, the dining scene in the US Virgin Islands is diverse and vibrant. In this chapter, we will provide you with essential tips for dining out, including how to choose a restaurant, order food, and pay the bill. Additionally, we will recommend some exceptional restaurants in different parts of the country, ensuring you have an unforgettable culinary experience.

Choosing a Restaurant:

1. Cuisine Variety: The US Virgin Islands boast a range of cuisines, from local Caribbean delicacies to international fare. Consider your preferences and explore the diverse options available before making a choice.

2. Location: Depending on your mood and preferences, you can opt for beachfront dining, romantic hilltop restaurants, or lively spots in town. The US Virgin Islands offer a plethora of settings to enhance your dining experience.

3. Reviews and Recommendations: Seek out reviews from locals and fellow travelers to get an authentic perspective on the restaurant's quality, service, and ambiance. Online review platforms and travel forums can provide valuable insights.

Ordering Food:

1. Local Specialties: Don't miss the opportunity to savor local delicacies like conch fritters, saltfish, and johnnycakes. These dishes are a true reflection of the island's cultural heritage and are sure to tantalize your taste buds.

2. Fresh Seafood: Being surrounded by pristine waters, the US Virgin Islands offer an abundance of fresh seafood options. Indulge in succulent lobster, red snapper, or mahi-mahi for an unforgettable dining experience.

3. Vegetarian and Vegan Options: Many restaurants in the US Virgin Islands cater to dietary preferences, offering a variety of vegetarian and vegan dishes. Don't hesitate to inquire about these options to ensure a satisfying meal.

Paying the Bill:

1. Tipping: Like in many parts of the United States, tipping is customary in the US Virgin Islands. It is customary to leave a gratuity of 15-20% of the total bill to acknowledge the service provided.

2. Payment Methods: Most restaurants accept major credit cards, but it's always a good idea to carry some cash for smaller establishments or in case of any technical difficulties with card payments.

Recommended Restaurants:

1. St. Thomas:

- The Mafolie Restaurant: Offering breathtaking views of Charlotte Amalie, this hilltop restaurant serves a fusion of Caribbean and international cuisine, accompanied by an extensive wine list.

- Gladys' Café: A local favorite, Gladys' Café serves mouthwatering Caribbean dishes such as curried goat and jerk chicken. Don't miss their famous banana daiquiris!

2. St. John:

- The Lime Inn: Located in Cruz Bay, The Lime Inn is renowned for its fresh seafood and creative fusion dishes. Their lobster bisque and coconut-crusted shrimp are highly recommended.

- Morgan's Mango: This tropical oasis offers a delectable blend of Caribbean and Latin American flavors. Try their signature dish, Mango Tango, a succulent combination of shrimp, scallops, and mango salsa.

3. St. Croix:

- Savant: Nestled in an enchanting courtyard, Savant offers a romantic dining experience with its candlelit tables and exquisite Mediterranean-inspired cuisine. Their homemade desserts are a must-try.

- Zion Modern Kitchen: Combining farm-to-table practices with Caribbean flair, Zion Modern Kitchen serves innovative dishes using locally sourced ingredients. Don't miss their Sunday brunch!

Conclusion:

Dining out in the United States Virgin Islands is an adventure for the senses. With a plethora of restaurants offering diverse cuisines, breathtaking views, and warm hospitality, you are sure to have an exceptional dining experience. By following our tips and exploring our recommended restaurants, you will embark on a culinary journey that will leave you craving for more.

Chapter 12: Food and Drink Festivals in United States Virgin Islands

Introduction:

The United States Virgin Islands is not only known for its stunning beaches and rich history but also for its vibrant culinary scene. Throughout the year, the islands come alive with a variety of food and drink festivals that celebrate the local flavors, traditions, and cultural diversity. This chapter will guide you through the calendar of major food and drink festivals in the United States Virgin Islands, offering a unique opportunity to indulge in delicious cuisine and experience the islands' vibrant atmosphere.

1. Mango Melee Festival:

Kicking off the festival season in the United States Virgin Islands is the highly anticipated Mango Melee Festival. Held annually in July at the St. George Village Botanical Garden on St. Croix, this festival pays homage to the island's most beloved fruit, the mango. Visitors can sample an array of mango-inspired dishes, from mango salsa to mango cocktails, while enjoying live music, local crafts, and educational exhibits about the fruit's cultivation. Don't miss the mango eating contest, where participants showcase their skills in devouring this tropical delight.

2. St. Thomas Food, Wine, and Rum Festival:

In November, food and drink enthusiasts flock to St. Thomas for the renowned Food, Wine, and Rum Festival. This four-day event showcases the culinary talents of local and international chefs, who create exquisite dishes using the freshest local ingredients. From gourmet dinners to wine tastings and mixology competitions, this festival offers a unique blend of flavors and experiences. Attendees can also enjoy live entertainment, cultural performances, and explore the island's vibrant nightlife.

3. St. John Festival:

The St. John Festival, held annually in June, is a month-long celebration of the island's rich culture, history, and gastronomy. As part of the festivities, the Food Fair takes center stage, offering a tantalizing array of local and international cuisines. From traditional Caribbean dishes to fusion creations, visitors can savor the flavors of the island while enjoying live music, dancing, and vibrant parades. This festival truly captures the spirit of St. John and its culinary traditions.

4. Taste of St. Croix:

Considered one of the premier food events in the Caribbean, the Taste of St. Croix attracts food lovers from around the world. This annual culinary extravaganza, held in April, brings together the island's top chefs, restaurants, and beverage purveyors for a night of gastronomic delight. Attendees can sample an impressive array of dishes, ranging from Caribbean classics to innovative creations, all paired with fine wines and spirits. The event also features live entertainment, cooking demonstrations, and a friendly chef competition that showcases the island's culinary talent.

5. Crucian Christmas Festival:

The Crucian Christmas Festival, held throughout December and January, is a cherished tradition in the United States Virgin Islands. As part of this festive celebration, the Food Fair serves as a culinary highlight, offering a wide variety of traditional holiday dishes. From succulent roasted pork to delectable pastries and local delicacies, visitors can experience the flavors of a Crucian Christmas. The fair also features live music, cultural performances, and a lively atmosphere that captures the spirit of the holiday season.

Conclusion:

The United States Virgin Islands is a paradise not only for beach lovers but also for food and drink enthusiasts. The calendar of major food and drink festivals offers a unique opportunity to explore the islands' culinary traditions, indulge in delicious cuisine, and immerse yourself in the vibrant atmosphere. From mango-inspired creations to gourmet dining experiences, these festivals showcase the diverse flavors and cultural heritage of the United States Virgin Islands. Don't miss the chance to savor the taste of the islands and create unforgettable memories during your visit.

Chapter 13: Getting to United States Virgin Islands

Introduction:

Welcome to Chapter 13 of our comprehensive tourist guide on the United States Virgin Islands! In this chapter, we will explore the different modes of transportation available for travelers to reach this enchanting destination. From planes soaring through the skies to ferries gliding across the crystal-clear waters, there are various options to suit every traveler's needs. So, let's dive in and discover the exciting ways to embark on your journey to the United States Virgin Islands!

1. By Plane:

The most common and convenient mode of transportation to the United States Virgin Islands is by air. The islands are served by two major airports: Cyril E. King Airport on St. Thomas and Henry E. Rohlsen Airport on St. Croix. These airports are well-connected to major cities in the United States, including Miami, New York, Atlanta, and Charlotte, making it easy for travelers to fly in from various locations. Several airlines offer direct flights to the United States Virgin Islands, ensuring a smooth and hassle-free journey.

2. By Train:

While the United States Virgin Islands do not have a train network, it's worth mentioning that some travelers may opt to take a train to a nearby city on the mainland and then continue their journey by air or sea. However, this option is not as common due to the availability of more direct modes of transportation.

3. By Bus:

Traveling to the United States Virgin Islands by bus is not possible as the islands are located in the Caribbean Sea. However, once you arrive on the islands, buses are a reliable and affordable means of transportation for exploring the different attractions within each island. Public buses, known as safaris operate on St. Thomas and St. John, while taxis and car rentals are also readily available.

4. By Car:

For those who prefer the freedom to explore at their own pace, traveling to the United States Virgin Islands by car is an option worth considering. However, it's important to note that driving to the islands is not possible due to their geographical location. Instead, visitors can rent a car upon arrival at the airports or take advantage of taxi services to navigate the islands comfortably.

5. By Ferry:

Another exciting way to reach the United States Virgin Islands is by ferry. Ferries operate between the islands, allowing travelers to experience the beauty of the Caribbean Sea while traveling. Regular ferry services connect St. Thomas, St. John, and St. Croix, providing a convenient means of island-hopping. Additionally, ferries also run between the British Virgin Islands and the United States Virgin Islands, offering travelers the opportunity to explore both island groups.

Conclusion:

In this chapter, we have explored the various modes of transportation available to travelers visiting the United States Virgin Islands. From the convenience of air travel to the charm of ferry rides, each option offers a unique experience. Whether you prefer the speed of a plane or the tranquility of a ferry, the United States Virgin Islands await your arrival. So, pack your bags, choose your preferred mode of transportation, and get ready to embark on a memorable journey to this Caribbean paradise!

Chapter 14: Exploring the United States Virgin Islands through Public Transportation

Introduction:

Welcome to Chapter 14 of our tourist guide, dedicated to helping you navigate the beautiful United States Virgin Islands using the various modes of public transportation available. From trains to buses and metros, this chapter will provide you with all the information you need to efficiently and conveniently explore the islands' captivating landscapes, vibrant cities, and historic sites. So, let's dive in and discover the unique public transportation options that await you in the US Virgin Islands.

1. The Island Hopper: A Comprehensive Overview

The United States Virgin Islands offer a well-connected and reliable public transportation system known as the Island Hopper. This comprehensive network of trains, buses, and metros ensures that visitors can easily access the islands' major attractions, towns, and cities. Whether you are a budget-conscious traveler or simply prefer to leave the driving to someone else, the Island Hopper is your gateway to an unforgettable island adventure.

2. Trains: A Scenic Journey

While the US Virgin Islands may not have traditional train systems, they offer an alternative mode of transportation that combines convenience and breathtaking views. Hop aboard the scenic railway tours available on St. Kitts and St. Croix. These historic trains take you on a journey through lush rainforests, picturesque coastal landscapes, and charming towns, providing an unforgettable perspective of the islands' natural beauty.

3. Buses: Navigating the Island's Heartbeat

The US Virgin Islands boast an extensive bus network that efficiently connects visitors to various destinations across the islands. Whether you're exploring the vibrant capital city of Charlotte Amalie on St. Thomas or soaking up the laid-back atmosphere of Christiansted on St. Croix, the buses provide a cost-effective and eco-friendly means of transportation. With regular schedules and affordable fares, buses offer a great way to immerse yourself in the local culture and interact with friendly locals.

4. Metros: Seamless City Exploration

For those exploring the bustling capital city of Charlotte Amalie on St. Thomas, the metro system is the ideal way to navigate its vibrant streets. The city's metro lines connect key landmarks, shopping districts, and cultural hotspots, allowing you to effortlessly explore the city's rich history and vibrant atmosphere. With -friendly maps and frequent service, the metro system ensures a seamless and enjoyable urban adventure.

5. The Capital City's Public Transportation Map

To assist you in your exploration of Charlotte Amalie, we have included a detailed map of the city's public transportation system. This map highlights the metro lines, bus routes, and key landmarks, providing you with a comprehensive guide to getting around the capital city with ease. From the iconic Blackbeard's Castle to the vibrant Main Street shopping district, this map will be your trusty companion as you delve into the heart of Charlotte Amalie.

Conclusion:

As you embark on your journey through the United States Virgin Islands, remember that public transportation is not only an efficient way to get around but also an opportunity to engage with the local culture and experience the islands from a unique perspective. Whether you choose to hop on a train, catch a bus, or ride the metro, the US Virgin Islands' public transportation system ensures that your exploration is seamless and memorable. So, sit back, relax, and let the Island Hopper take you on an unforgettable adventure through these enchanting Caribbean gems.

Chapter 15: Types of Accommodation in United States Virgin Islands

Introduction:

When planning your visit to the United States Virgin Islands, one of the key aspects to consider is the type of accommodation that will suit your needs and preferences. The islands offer a diverse range of options, from luxurious hotels to cozy guesthouses and unique Airbnbs. This chapter will guide you through the various types of accommodation available, ensuring you make an informed decision that enhances your stay in this tropical paradise.

1. Luxurious Hotels:

The United States Virgin Islands boast a selection of world-class hotels that cater to those seeking the ultimate in comfort and luxury. From elegant beachfront resorts to boutique hotels nestled in lush tropical gardens, these accommodations offer a wide range of amenities such as spas, fine dining restaurants, private pools, and breathtaking ocean views. Some notable examples include The Ritz-Carlton, St. Thomas, and The Buccaneer in St. Croix.

2. Charming Guesthouses:

For a more intimate and authentic experience, consider staying at one of the many charming guesthouses scattered throughout the islands. These accommodations provide a cozy and homely atmosphere, often run by friendly local hosts who are eager to share their knowledge of the area. Guesthouses can be found in both urban and rural settings, offering a unique opportunity to immerse yourself in the local culture. The Mafolie Hotel in St. Thomas and Coconuts Villa in St. John are excellent choices for those seeking a personalized experience.

3. Budget-Friendly Hostels:

If you are a budget-conscious traveler or enjoy meeting fellow adventurers, hostels in the United States Virgin Islands can be an excellent choice. These accommodations offer shared dormitory-style rooms, communal spaces, and often organize social activities for guests. While they may lack some of the amenities of luxury hotels, hostels provide a vibrant and lively atmosphere, making them perfect for solo travelers or groups of friends. The Virgin Islands Campground in St. John and The St. Thomas Hostel are popular options for budget travelers.

4. Unique Airbnbs:

For those seeking a more personalized and independent experience, renting an Airbnb can be an ideal choice. The United States Virgin Islands offer a wide range of unique properties, from cozy cottages and beachfront villas to charming apartments in historic buildings. Staying in an Airbnb allows you to live like a local, providing the freedom to explore the islands at your own pace and enjoy the comforts of a home away from home. From Cruz Bay in St. John to Christiansted in St. Croix, there are countless Airbnb options to suit every taste and budget.

Conclusion:

Choosing the right type of accommodation for your visit to the United States Virgin Islands is essential to ensure a memorable and enjoyable stay. Whether you prefer the luxury of hotels, the charm of guesthouses, the affordability of hostels, or the independence of Airbnbs, the islands offer a diverse range of options to cater to your needs. Consider your budget, desired level of comfort, and the experiences you wish to have while exploring these beautiful Caribbean islands.

Chapter 16: Tips for Staying in the United States Virgin Islands

The United States Virgin Islands (USVI) is a tropical paradise located in the Caribbean Sea. With its stunning beaches, vibrant culture, and rich history, it's no wonder that it attracts millions of tourists each year. However, to ensure a smooth and enjoyable stay, it's essential to be well-prepared. In this chapter, we will provide you with valuable tips for booking accommodation, getting around, and staying safe during your visit to the USVI.

1. Booking Accommodation:

a. Research and compare: Before booking your accommodation, take the time to research and compare different options. Consider factors such as location, amenities, and reviews from previous guests. Websites like TripAdvisor and Booking.com can be useful resources for finding the perfect place to stay.

b. Book in advance: To secure the best deals and availability, it's advisable to book your accommodation well in advance, especially during peak travel seasons. This will help you avoid any last-minute stress and ensure you have a comfortable place to stay.

2. Getting Around:

a. Renting a car: Renting a car is highly recommended for exploring the USVI. It provides the flexibility to visit various attractions at your own pace. However, keep in mind that driving is on the left side of the road, and you will need to obtain a temporary driving permit upon arrival.

b. Public transportation: If you prefer not to drive, public transportation options are available. Taxis, buses, and ferries are convenient and reliable modes of transport within and between the islands. Make sure to check the schedules in advance to plan your trips accordingly.

3. Staying Safe:

a. Be cautious of your surroundings: While the USVI is generally safe, it's essential to remain vigilant and aware of your surroundings, particularly in crowded tourist areas. Avoid displaying expensive belongings and be cautious of pickpockets.

b. Follow local regulations: Familiarize yourself with local laws and regulations to ensure you have a trouble-free stay. For example, it is illegal to use marijuana in the USVI, and drinking alcohol in public places is prohibited.

c. Protect yourself from the sun: The Caribbean sun can be intense, so it's crucial to protect yourself from harmful UV rays. Apply sunscreen regularly, wear a hat and sunglasses, and seek shade during the peak hours of the day.

By following these tips, you can make the most of your stay in the United States Virgin Islands. Remember to plan ahead, stay informed, and embrace the beauty and culture that this enchanting destination has to offer. Enjoy your time in the USVI, and may it be filled with unforgettable memories!

Chapter 17: Must-see Attractions in United States Virgin Islands

Welcome to the United States Virgin Islands, a tropical paradise in the Caribbean that offers a perfect blend of stunning natural beauty, rich history, and vibrant culture. In this chapter, we will explore the top 10 must-see attractions that will leave you in awe of these breathtaking islands. Get ready to embark on an unforgettable journey!

1. Magens Bay Beach: Start your adventure by visiting one of the most picturesque beaches in the world. With its crystal-clear turquoise waters and soft white sand, Magens Bay Beach is a true paradise for beach lovers. Take a dip, soak up the sun, or simply relax under the swaying palm trees.

2. Charlotte Amalie: Explore the historic capital of the United States Virgin Islands, Charlotte Amalie. Walk along the cobblestone streets and marvel at the colonial architecture. Don't miss the chance to visit Blackbeard's Castle, a 17th-century fortress that offers panoramic views of the city and the harbor.

3. Trunk Bay: Venture to St. John Island and discover the captivating beauty of Trunk Bay. This world-famous beach is renowned for its crystal-clear waters, vibrant coral reefs, and an underwater snorkeling trail. Immerse yourself in the colorful marine life and be amazed by the natural wonders that lie beneath the surface.

4. Virgin Islands National Park: Escape to the lush wilderness of the Virgin Islands National Park, covering over 60% of St. John Island. Hike through the tropical rainforest, swim in pristine waters, and encounter diverse wildlife. Don't forget to visit the historic ruins of sugar plantations, a reminder of the island's past.

5. Coral World Ocean Park: Dive into an underwater adventure at Coral World Ocean Park on St. Thomas Island. Explore the vibrant marine life through an underwater observatory tower or get up close

and personal with sea turtles, sharks, and stingrays in interactive exhibits. It's an educational and thrilling experience for all ages.

6. Buck Island Reef National Monument: Hop on a boat and head to Buck Island Reef National Monument, located just off the coast of St. Croix Island. This protected marine park is home to an extraordinary underwater trail, where you can snorkel among colorful coral reefs and encounter tropical fish in their natural habitat.

7. Caneel Bay: Indulge in luxury and tranquility at Caneel Bay, a secluded resort nestled within the Virgin Islands National Park on St. John Island. With its pristine beaches, lush tropical gardens, and world-class amenities, this exclusive retreat offers a truly unforgettable experience.

8. Salt River Bay National Historical Park and Ecological Preserve: Explore the historical and ecological wonders of Salt River Bay on St. Croix Island. This unique park is a combination of natural beauty and historical significance. Take a guided kayak tour through the bioluminescent bay and learn about the indigenous Taino people who once inhabited the area.

9. Annaberg Plantation: Step back in time and visit the ruins of Annaberg Plantation on St. John Island. This former sugar plantation provides a glimpse into the island's colonial past. Explore the restored windmill, slave quarters, and other structures while learning about the harsh realities of plantation life.

10. Hassel Island: Conclude your journey by visiting Hassel Island, a small uninhabited island located in the Charlotte Amalie harbor. Take a scenic hike to the ruins of Fort Willoughby, a historic military fort, and enjoy panoramic views of the surrounding islands. This hidden gem is a perfect spot to unwind and reflect on your adventures.

As you explore these must-see attractions in the United States Virgin Islands, you'll discover a world of natural wonders, rich history, and vibrant culture. Each destination offers a unique experience that will leave a lasting impression on your heart. So, pack your bags, embrace the island vibes, and get ready for an unforgettable journey in this Caribbean paradise.

Chapter 18: Natural Wonders of the United States Virgin Islands

45

Welcome to Chapter 18 of our tourist guide, where we will explore the breathtaking natural wonders that adorn the United States Virgin Islands. This tropical paradise, located in the Caribbean Sea, is renowned for its pristine beaches, crystal-clear waters, and diverse ecosystems. Get ready to be captivated by the top 10 natural wonders that await you in this enchanting destination.

1. Trunk Bay: Our journey begins at Trunk Bay, a true gem of the Virgin Islands National Park. This stunning beach boasts powdery white sand, vibrant coral reefs, and an underwater trail that allows visitors to explore the marine life up close. Immerse yourself in the tranquility of this paradise and let the beauty of Trunk Bay leave you in awe.

2. The Baths: Prepare to be amazed by The Baths, a unique geological formation found on the island of Virgin Gorda. Massive granite boulders create a labyrinth of caves, tunnels, and pools, forming an otherworldly landscape. Take a leisurely stroll through this natural wonder and discover hidden grottos and secluded beaches along the way.

3. Magens Bay: Nestled on the island of St. Thomas, Magens Bay is a picturesque horseshoe-shaped beach renowned for its crystal-clear turquoise waters and lush green surroundings. This idyllic spot offers a perfect blend of tranquility and natural beauty, making it a must-visit destination for nature enthusiasts.

4. Salt River Bay National Historical Park and Ecological Preserve: Delve into the rich history and ecological diversity of the Salt River Bay National Historical Park and Ecological Preserve. This protected area encompasses mangrove forests, coral reefs, and archaeological sites, providing a unique opportunity to explore the region's past while immersing yourself in its natural wonders.

5. Buck Island Reef National Monument: Embark on an unforgettable snorkeling adventure at the Buck Island Reef National Monument. This marine paradise, located just off the coast of St. Croix,

boasts an underwater trail that leads you through vibrant coral gardens and a diverse array of marine life, including sea turtles and tropical fish.

6. Caneel Bay: Situated on the island of St. John, Caneel Bay offers a serene escape surrounded by lush tropical forests and pristine beaches. This secluded natural wonder is perfect for snorkeling, hiking, or simply unwinding amidst the breathtaking beauty of its unspoiled landscapes.

7. Coral World Ocean Park: Dive into the wonders of the underwater world at Coral World Ocean Park. Located on St. Thomas, this marine park offers unique opportunities to observe and interact with a variety of marine creatures, including sharks, stingrays, and sea turtles. Explore the park's underwater observatory or take a walk through the tropical gardens for an unforgettable experience.

8. Virgin Islands Coral Reef National Monument: Discover the vibrant and diverse coral reefs that make up the Virgin Islands Coral Reef National Monument. This protected area spans over 12,708 acres and is home to an abundance of marine life, including colorful coral formations, tropical fish, and endangered species. Snorkel or dive in these pristine waters to witness the wonders of this underwater paradise.

9. Annaberg Plantation: Immerse yourself in the cultural and natural heritage of the United States Virgin Islands at the Annaberg Plantation. Located within the Virgin Islands National Park on St. John, this historic site offers a glimpse into the island's colonial past and its connection to the natural environment. Explore the ruins of the sugar plantation and enjoy panoramic views of the surrounding landscapes.

10. Honeymoon Beach: Conclude your journey at Honeymoon Beach, a hidden gem on the island of Water Island. This secluded paradise offers pristine white sand, calm turquoise waters, and lush greenery, providing the perfect setting for a romantic escape or a peaceful day in nature.

As you explore the natural wonders of the United States Virgin Islands, remember to respect and preserve these delicate ecosystems. Take nothing but photographs, leave nothing but footprints, and cherish the memories of this extraordinary destination.

Chapter 19: Historical and Cultural Sites in the United States Virgin Islands

The United States Virgin Islands, a stunning Caribbean paradise, is not only known for its pristine beaches and crystal-clear waters but also for its rich historical and cultural heritage. This chapter will take you on a journey to the top 10 historical and cultural sites in these beautiful islands, where you can explore the fascinating stories and traditions that have shaped their unique identity.

1. Fort Christian, St. Thomas:

Located in Charlotte Amalie, the capital city of the US Virgin Islands, Fort Christian is a historic landmark that dates back to the 17th century. This well-preserved fortress served as a military stronghold and later transformed into a museum, showcasing artifacts and exhibits that depict the island's colonial past.

2. Blackbeard's Castle, St. Thomas:

Perched atop a hill in Charlotte Amalie, Blackbeard's Castle offers panoramic views of the harbor and the surrounding islands. Although the infamous pirate Blackbeard never actually resided here, the tower-like structure and the nearby historic mansions provide visitors with a glimpse into the island's pirate lore and Danish colonial history.

3. Estate Whim Plantation Museum, St. Croix:

Step back in time at the Estate Whim Plantation Museum, a restored 18th-century sugar plantation on St. Croix. This living museum provides a comprehensive understanding of the island's sugar industry, African heritage, and the lives of the enslaved people who worked on the plantation.

4. Christiansted National Historic Site, St. Croix:

Explore the charming town of Christiansted, a designated National Historic Site, and wander its cobblestone streets lined with colorful Danish colonial buildings. Visit Fort Christiansvaern, a well-preserved fortification that guarded the town during the colonial era, and learn about the island's Danish, African, and West Indian influences.

5. Cinnamon Bay Archaeological Site, St. John:

Immerse yourself in the indigenous history of the Virgin Islands at the Cinnamon Bay Archaeological Site. This site showcases the remains of a pre-Columbian village, providing insights into the lives of the Taino people who inhabited the island before European colonization.

6. Frederiksted, St. Croix:

Discover the vibrant town of Frederiksted, known for its colorful Victorian architecture and historical landmarks. Visit Fort Frederik, a Danish fortress built in the 18th century, and explore the town's museums, art galleries, and local crafts markets.

7. Hassel Island, St. Thomas:

Embark on a journey to Hassel Island, a small uninhabited island off the coast of St. Thomas. This historical gem is home to ruins of military fortifications, including Fort Willoughby and Fort Shipley, which played significant roles in protecting the harbor during the colonial era.

8. St. John's Church, St. John:

Located in Cruz Bay, St. John's Church is one of the oldest Anglican churches in the Caribbean. This historic church, built in 1750, showcases beautiful stained glass windows and offers a peaceful sanctuary for reflection and worship.

9. Salt River Bay National Historical Park and Ecological Preserve, St. Croix:

Explore the natural and historical wonders of Salt River Bay, a site of great ecological and cultural significance. This national park preserves the area where Christopher Columbus made his second voyage to the New World and provides opportunities for kayaking, snorkeling, and hiking.

10. The Virgin Islands National Park, St. John:

Encompassing over 60% of the island of St. John, the Virgin Islands National Park is a treasure trove of natural beauty and historical sites. Discover ancient petroglyphs at Reef Bay, explore historic plantation ruins, and hike through lush forests to breathtaking beaches such as Trunk Bay and Cinnamon Bay.

As you explore these top 10 historical and cultural sites in the United States Virgin Islands, you will gain a deeper appreciation for the islands' diverse heritage and the people who have shaped their past. From colonial forts to ancient indigenous sites, each location offers a unique glimpse into the rich tapestry of the Virgin Islands' history and culture.

Chapter 20: Museums and Art Galleries in the United States Virgin Islands

Introduction:

The United States Virgin Islands is not only a tropical paradise with stunning beaches and crystal-clear waters but also a hub of culture and art. This chapter will guide you through the top 10 museums and art galleries in the US Virgin Islands, providing a unique and truthful insight into the rich artistic heritage of these islands.

1. The Virgin Islands Museum:

Located in the heart of Charlotte Amalie, the Virgin Islands Museum is a must-visit for history enthusiasts. This museum offers a comprehensive overview of the islands' past, showcasing artifacts, photographs, and exhibits that highlight the region's cultural and historical significance.

2. The Caribbean Museum Center for the Arts:

Situated in the charming town of Frederiksted, the Caribbean Museum Center for the Arts is a vibrant space dedicated to promoting contemporary Caribbean art. Visitors can explore thought-provoking exhibitions, attend workshops, and engage with local artists, gaining a deeper understanding of the region's artistic expressions.

3. The St. Thomas Historical Trust Museum:

Nestled within a historic building in St. Thomas, the St. Thomas Historical Trust Museum is a treasure trove of local history. From the island's colonial past to the struggles for emancipation, this museum offers a comprehensive look into the evolution of St. Thomas, showcasing artifacts and documents that bring the stories to life.

4. The Mango Tango Art Gallery:

Located in Christiansted, the Mango Tango Art Gallery is a must-visit for art lovers seeking a taste of the vibrant local art scene. Featuring a diverse collection of paintings, sculptures, and mixed media works, this gallery showcases the talent and creativity of both local and international artists.

5. The Estate Whim Museum:

Immerse yourself in the island's sugar plantation history by visiting the Estate Whim Museum on St. Croix. This living museum allows visitors to explore the beautifully restored Great House, sugar mill, and slave quarters, providing a unique glimpse into the island's colonial past.

6. The Tillett Gardens and Art Center:

Nestled in the hills of St. Thomas, the Tillett Gardens and Art Center is a hidden gem for art enthusiasts. This creative hub features a collection of artist studios, galleries, and shops, offering visitors the opportunity to meet local artists, purchase unique artworks, and witness the creative process firsthand.

7. The Seven Arches Museum:

Situated in Christiansted, the Seven Arches Museum is a captivating space dedicated to preserving the Virgin Islands' cultural heritage. This museum showcases the island's African and Danish influences through its extensive collection of artifacts, including traditional crafts, artwork, and historical documents.

8. The Art of Recycling Gallery:

Located in Cruz Bay, the Art of Recycling Gallery is a one-of-a-kind space that promotes sustainability and creativity. This gallery features artwork created from recycled materials, showcasing the talent of local artists while raising awareness about environmental issues.

9. The Elaine Ione Sprauve Library and Museum:

Nestled in the picturesque town of Coral Bay, the Elaine Ione Sprauve Library and Museum is a cultural gem. This museum provides a fascinating insight into the island's history and culture, housing a collection of historical documents, photographs, and artifacts that highlight the unique heritage of St. John.

10. The Mongoose Junction Galleries:

Situated in Cruz Bay, the Mongoose Junction Galleries offer a diverse range of artistic expressions, from contemporary paintings to traditional crafts. With numerous galleries to explore, visitors can immerse themselves in the vibrant local art scene, finding that perfect piece to take home as a memento of their trip.

Conclusion:

The United States Virgin Islands is not only a tropical paradise but also a haven for art and culture. From museums showcasing the islands' rich history to galleries promoting contemporary Caribbean art, there is something for every art enthusiast to explore. Immerse yourself in the artistic heritage of the US Virgin Islands and uncover the unique stories behind each masterpiece.

Chapter 21: Religious Sites in United States Virgin Islands

Introduction:

The United States Virgin Islands, nestled in the Caribbean Sea, is not only renowned for its stunning beaches and vibrant culture but also for its rich religious heritage. This chapter will take you on a spiritual journey, exploring the top ten religious sites that offer a glimpse into the diverse faiths and beliefs of the island's inhabitants. From historic churches to sacred monuments, prepare to be inspired by the religious sites of the United States Virgin Islands.

1. St. Thomas Synagogue, Charlotte Amalie:

As the second-oldest synagogue in the Western Hemisphere, the St. Thomas Synagogue is a testament to the Jewish community's enduring presence on the island. Built in 1833, this beautiful synagogue showcases stunning Gothic Revival architecture and houses a museum that delves into the Jewish history of the Virgin Islands.

2. St. George Village Botanical Garden, St. Croix:

Nestled within the lush landscapes of St. Croix, the St. George Village Botanical Garden offers visitors a serene retreat where spirituality intertwines with nature. Explore the garden's various religious statues and meditation spots, which represent different faiths and provide a tranquil space for introspection.

3. Frederick Lutheran Church, Charlotte Amalie:

Dating back to the 17th century, the Frederick Lutheran Church is one of the oldest religious sites in the United States Virgin Islands. This historic church, with its distinctive red roof, offers a glimpse into the island's Danish colonial past and serves as a place of worship for the local Lutheran community.

4. Cathedral of Saints Peter and Paul, St. Thomas:

Situated in the heart of Charlotte Amalie, the Cathedral of Saints Peter and Paul stands as a prominent symbol of Catholicism on the island. This grand cathedral, with its awe-inspiring architecture and breathtaking stained glass windows, welcomes both locals and visitors to experience the beauty of Catholic worship.

5. Hassel Island, St. Thomas:

Hassel Island, a small uninhabited island off the coast of St. Thomas, holds significant historical and religious importance. Explore the ruins of the Danish West India and Guinea Company Warehouse, which once served as a place of worship for enslaved Africans, offering a glimpse into the island's complex past.

6. The Church of God of Prophecy, St. John:

Located in the picturesque town of Cruz Bay, The Church of God of Prophecy is a vibrant hub of worship and spiritual growth. Join the local congregation in their uplifting services, where music, prayer, and fellowship create a welcoming atmosphere for people of all backgrounds.

7. Annaberg Sugar Plantation, St. John:

While primarily known for its historical significance, the Annaberg Sugar Plantation also holds religious importance. Visit the ruins of the plantation's chapel, where enslaved Africans found solace and strength through their faith. This site serves as a reminder of the resilience and spirituality of those who endured challenging times.

8. Frederick Evangelical Lutheran Church, St. Croix:

Step into the Frederick Evangelical Lutheran Church, located in the charming town of Frederiksted, and discover its rich history and architectural beauty. This church, founded in 1755, showcases a blend of Danish and Gothic Revival styles, providing a serene space for worship and reflection.

9. Emmaus Moravian Church, St. Thomas:

Nestled in the picturesque village of Nazareth, the Emmaus Moravian Church is a place of tranquility and spiritual connection.

Attend a service and immerse yourself in the harmonious melodies of the Moravian choir, experience the warmth of their hospitality, and learn about the Moravian traditions that have shaped the island's culture.

10. Blackbeard's Castle, St. Thomas:

While primarily known for its pirate history, Blackbeard's Castle also holds religious significance. Ascend the historic tower and discover the hidden Lutheran Church, which served as a place of worship for the Danish soldiers stationed at the castle. Take in the breathtaking views of Charlotte Amalie while reflecting on the island's intriguing past.

Conclusion:

The United States Virgin Islands' religious sites offer a unique opportunity to explore the island's diverse spiritual landscape. From synagogues and churches to plantations and hidden chapels, each site tells a story of faith, resilience, and cultural heritage. Embark on this spiritual journey and discover the captivating religious sites that make the United States Virgin Islands a truly remarkable destination.

Chapter 22: Outdoor Activities in the United States Virgin Islands

Introduction:

Welcome to the United States Virgin Islands, a tropical paradise in the Caribbean that offers a plethora of outdoor activities for adventure enthusiasts and nature lovers alike. Whether you are seeking adrenaline-pumping experiences or simply wish to immerse yourself in the stunning natural beauty, this chapter will guide you through the top 10 outdoor activities in the US Virgin Islands.

1. Snorkeling and Scuba Diving:

Immerse yourself in the crystal-clear turquoise waters surrounding the US Virgin Islands and discover a world teeming with vibrant coral reefs, colorful tropical fish, and mesmerizing marine life. Explore popular snorkeling spots like Trunk Bay on St. John or venture deeper into the ocean with scuba diving excursions to famous sites like the Wreck of the Rhone.

2. Hiking in Virgin Islands National Park:

Embark on a hiking adventure through the lush Virgin Islands National Park on St. John, covering over 7,000 acres of unspoiled beauty. Follow scenic trails such as the Reef Bay Trail, which leads you through dense forests, ancient petroglyphs, and cascading waterfalls, offering breathtaking views along the way.

3. Kayaking in the Mangrove Lagoons:

Paddle through the serene mangrove lagoons of St. Thomas or St. Croix, where you can witness the delicate ecosystem up close. Glide through narrow waterways, spot native wildlife such as herons and turtles, and learn about the importance of preserving these unique habitats.

4. Zip-lining through the Rainforest:

Get your heart racing as you zip-line through the lush rainforests of St. Thomas. Soar above the treetops, taking in panoramic views of the island's stunning landscapes while experiencing an exhilarating adventure that combines adrenaline and nature.

5. Horseback Riding on the Beach:

Saddle up and embark on a horseback riding tour along the pristine beaches of St. Croix. Enjoy the rhythmic sound of hooves hitting the sand as you explore the coastline, taking in the breathtaking views of the Caribbean Sea and feeling the warm ocean breeze against your skin.

6. Sailing and Yachting:

Take to the open waters and set sail on a yacht or catamaran, exploring the US Virgin Islands from a different perspective. Enjoy the freedom of cruising along the coastline, stopping at secluded coves, and snorkeling in hidden bays, all while basking in the Caribbean sun.

7. Deep-Sea Fishing:

For those seeking a thrilling angling experience, the US Virgin Islands offer excellent deep-sea fishing opportunities. Charter a boat and head out to the deep waters, where you can try your luck at catching marlin, mahi-mahi, or tuna, creating memories that will last a lifetime.

8. Stand-Up Paddleboarding:

Test your balance and core strength with a stand-up paddleboarding adventure in the calm bays of St. Thomas or St. John. Glide over the turquoise waters, explore hidden coves, and enjoy the tranquility of being surrounded by the stunning coastal scenery.

9. Rock Climbing in the Virgin Gorda:

Venture to the nearby British Virgin Islands and explore the rugged cliffs of Virgin Gorda, known for its world-class rock climbing opportunities. Challenge yourself on various routes, scale towering cliffs, and be rewarded with breathtaking views of the surrounding islands.

10. Birdwatching in Salt River Bay National Historical Park:

Discover the diverse bird species that inhabit the Salt River Bay National Historical Park on St. Croix. Grab your binoculars and embark on a birdwatching expedition, spotting magnificent frigatebirds, colorful parrots, and other unique avian species in their natural habitat.

Conclusion:

The United States Virgin Islands offer a wide range of outdoor activities that cater to all interests and levels of adventure. From exploring underwater wonders to hiking through lush forests and engaging in thrilling water sports, the US Virgin Islands are a paradise for outdoor enthusiasts. So, pack your bags, put on your sunscreen, and get ready to make unforgettable memories in this tropical haven.

Chapter 23: Shopping in United States Virgin Islands

As you explore the breathtaking beauty of the United States Virgin Islands, don't forget to indulge in the unique shopping experiences that await you. From local crafts to high-end boutiques, the US Virgin Islands offer a diverse range of shopping opportunities. In this chapter, we will guide you through the best places to shop and what to buy during your visit.

1. Charlotte Amalie - A Shopper's Paradise:

Start your shopping adventure in the vibrant capital city of Charlotte Amalie on the island of St. Thomas. This bustling town is renowned for its duty-free shopping, making it a haven for bargain hunters. The Main Street, known as Dronningens Gade, is lined with an array of shops, from luxury brands to local boutiques. Here, you can find exquisite jewelry, watches, perfumes, and designer clothing at significantly lower prices than back home.

2. Yacht Haven Grande - Luxury Shopping:

For those seeking a more upscale shopping experience, Yacht Haven Grande is the place to be. Located in Charlotte Amalie, this marina features an impressive selection of high-end boutiques and designer stores. Indulge in a shopping spree at renowned brands such as Louis Vuitton, Gucci, and Tiffany & Co. While the prices may be higher, the quality and exclusivity of the items make it worth the splurge.

3. Mongoose Junction - Island Chic:

On the picturesque island of St. John, Mongoose Junction offers a charming and unique shopping experience. This open-air shopping center showcases local artists and craftsmen, providing a wide range of handmade jewelry, clothing, and artwork. Explore the various boutiques and galleries, and take home a piece of the island's culture and creativity.

4. Wharfside Village - Caribbean Souvenirs:

Located in Cruz Bay, St. John, Wharfside Village is a delightful shopping destination for those looking for Caribbean souvenirs. Browse through the colorful shops and stalls, offering an assortment of island-inspired gifts, t-shirts, and trinkets. Don't miss the chance to pick up some local spices, hot sauces, and rum to bring the flavors of the US Virgin Islands back home with you.

5. Christiansted - Historic Shopping:

Venture to the island of St. Croix and immerse yourself in the rich history of Christiansted. This charming town is home to numerous boutiques and art galleries, perfect for those seeking unique treasures. Explore the historic streets and discover handcrafted jewelry, local artwork, and traditional Caribbean crafts. Take a stroll along the boardwalk and enjoy the scenic views while you shop.

6. Local Markets - Fresh Produce and Handicrafts:

For an authentic taste of the US Virgin Islands, visit the local markets scattered throughout the islands. These markets offer an opportunity to connect with the locals and experience the vibrant culture firsthand. Sample fresh tropical fruits, taste local delicacies, and browse through stalls selling handmade crafts and artwork. The colorful and lively atmosphere will leave you with lasting memories of your visit.

Remember, when shopping in the United States Virgin Islands, be sure to check the duty-free allowances and restrictions of your home country. Take advantage of the duty-free status to save on luxury items and souvenirs. Enjoy the diverse shopping experiences that the US Virgin Islands have to offer, and bring home a piece of paradise to cherish forever.

Chapter 24: Nightlife in United States Virgin Islands

Introduction:

Welcome to the vibrant and exciting nightlife of the United States Virgin Islands! When the sun sets, the islands come alive with a variety of entertainment options that cater to all tastes and preferences. From lively beach bars to elegant lounges, this chapter will guide you through the best places to go out at night in the US Virgin Islands, along with some valuable tips for enjoying the nightlife to the fullest.

1. Charlotte Amalie: The Heartbeat of the Night

As the capital and largest city of the US Virgin Islands, Charlotte Amalie offers a bustling nightlife scene. The historic streets are lined with bars, clubs, and restaurants, creating an energetic atmosphere. Head to Main Street and Waterfront for a mix of local hotspots and international venues, where you can enjoy live music, dance the night away, or simply relax with a cocktail in hand.

2. Cruz Bay: A Laid-Back Evening

On the island of St. John, Cruz Bay is known for its laid-back and friendly vibe. The town offers a range of bars and pubs where you can unwind and socialize with both locals and fellow travelers. Visit one of the beachfront establishments to enjoy stunning sunset views while sipping on a refreshing tropical drink. Don't miss the chance to try some local rum, a specialty of the US Virgin Islands.

3. Red Hook: A Partygoer's Paradise

Located on the eastern end of the island of St. Thomas, Red Hook is a popular destination for those seeking a lively nightlife experience. This vibrant area is packed with bars, nightclubs, and restaurants that cater to all tastes. Whether you're looking for a relaxed evening with live music or a high-energy dance floor, Red Hook has it all. Make sure to try some of the delicious seafood dishes served in the area's restaurants before hitting the town.

4. Beach Bars: Where Fun Meets Relaxation

No visit to the US Virgin Islands would be complete without experiencing the unique beach bar culture. These laid-back establishments, often located right on the sand, offer a perfect blend of fun and relaxation. Grab a seat at one of the beachfront bars, order a tropical cocktail, and enjoy the sound of the waves while socializing with locals and fellow travelers. Some popular beach bars include The Beach Bar on St. John and Duffy's Love Shack on St. Thomas.

5. Tips for Enjoying the Nightlife:

a. Safety First: As with any nightlife experience, it's important to prioritize your safety. Always be aware of your surroundings and avoid walking alone in unfamiliar areas at night.

b. Local Recommendations: Don't hesitate to ask locals for their favorite spots. They often know the hidden gems that may not be as well-known to tourists.

c. Dress Code: While the US Virgin Islands have a relaxed atmosphere, some venues may have specific dress codes. It's a good idea to check in advance to ensure you're appropriately dressed for the night out.

d. Transportation: Plan your transportation in advance, especially if you're visiting different islands. Taxis or designated drivers are recommended to ensure a safe return to your accommodation.

Conclusion:

The nightlife in the United States Virgin Islands offers a diverse and exciting experience for visitors. From the vibrant streets of Charlotte Amalie to the laid-back beach bars, there is something for everyone to enjoy. Remember to embrace the local culture, stay safe, and make the most of your nights in this tropical paradise.

Chapter 25: Festivals and Events in United States Virgin Islands

Introduction:

The United States Virgin Islands is not only known for its stunning beaches and crystal-clear waters but also for its vibrant culture and lively festivals. Throughout the year, locals and tourists alike gather to celebrate the rich heritage and traditions of this Caribbean paradise. In this chapter, we will explore the calendar of major festivals and events in the United States Virgin Islands, offering you an unforgettable experience of the island's unique celebrations.

1. Carnival - A Celebration of Life and Culture:

The highlight of the festival calendar in the United States Virgin Islands is undoubtedly Carnival. Held annually in April, this vibrant event brings together locals and visitors for a month-long celebration of music, dance, and culture. The streets come alive with colorful parades, calypso music, and extravagant costumes. Immerse yourself in the infectious energy and revel in the spirit of unity and joy that permeates the air during this festive time.

2. Food and Culture Festival:

For those with a passion for tantalizing their taste buds, the Food and Culture Festival is an event not to be missed. Held in June, this festival showcases the diversity of Caribbean cuisine, with local chefs and food vendors offering a delectable array of dishes. From mouthwatering seafood to traditional island delicacies, this festival is a culinary delight that allows you to savor the flavors of the Virgin Islands while enjoying live music and cultural performances.

3. St. Thomas International Regatta:

For sailing enthusiasts, the St. Thomas International Regatta is a premier event that attracts participants from around the world. Held annually in March, this thrilling regatta showcases the beauty of the

Virgin Islands' azure waters and challenges sailors with its competitive races. Whether you are a seasoned sailor or a spectator, this event offers an exhilarating experience and an opportunity to witness world-class yachting in a breathtaking setting.

4. Crucian Christmas Festival:

Experience the magic of the holiday season in the United States Virgin Islands by attending the Crucian Christmas Festival. Taking place in December, this festival blends traditional Christmas festivities with the vibrant culture of the islands. Enjoy parades, live music, local crafts, and delicious Caribbean cuisine as you immerse yourself in the festive spirit. The highlight of the festival is the J'ouvert, a lively street party that marks the beginning of the Christmas season with dancing, music, and joyful revelry.

5. Mango Melee:

If you happen to visit the United States Virgin Islands in July, make sure to attend the Mango Melee festival. Celebrating the island's most beloved fruit, this event offers a unique opportunity to indulge in all things mango. From mango tastings and cooking demonstrations to mango-themed competitions, this festival is a fruity paradise for both locals and visitors. Enjoy the tropical ambiance, live entertainment, and the chance to sample a variety of mouthwatering mango creations.

Conclusion:

The United States Virgin Islands is a destination that knows how to celebrate life, culture, and traditions. Whether you're a music lover, a food enthusiast, or a sailing enthusiast, the calendar of festivals and events in the Virgin Islands offers something for everyone. Immerse yourself in the vibrant atmosphere, embrace the local customs, and create lasting memories as you partake in these unique celebrations. Plan your visit accordingly, and get ready to be swept away by the infectious spirit of the United States Virgin Islands.

Chapter 26: Activities for Couples in the United States Virgin Islands

Introduction:

The United States Virgin Islands is an idyllic destination for couples seeking a romantic getaway. With its pristine beaches, crystal-clear turquoise waters, and breathtaking landscapes, this Caribbean paradise offers a plethora of activities that are perfect for creating lasting memories with your loved one. In this chapter, we will explore the top 10 most romantic activities for couples in the United States Virgin Islands.

1. Sunset Sailboat Cruise:

Embark on a sunset sailboat cruise and let the gentle sea breeze caress your skin as you watch the sun dip below the horizon. Toast to your love with a glass of champagne while enjoying the panoramic views of the islands and the vibrant colors of the sky.

2. Private Beach Picnic:

Escape to a secluded beach and indulge in a private picnic with your significant other. Bask in the sun, take a dip in the azure waters, and savor a delicious spread of local delicacies. This intimate experience will create an unforgettable memory for both of you.

3. Couples Massage on the Beach:

Pamper yourselves with a couples massage on the beach, where the rhythmic sound of the waves will enhance your relaxation. Let skilled therapists melt away your stress as you and your partner unwind together in this serene setting.

4. Underwater Snorkeling Adventure:

Dive into the vibrant underwater world of the United States Virgin Islands and explore the colorful coral reefs hand in hand with your loved one. Witness the beauty of marine life as you snorkel together, creating a shared experience that is both romantic and awe-inspiring.

5. Sunset Horseback Ride:

Embark on a romantic horseback ride along the beach at sunset. As you and your partner trot along the shoreline, feel the connection between nature, the horses, and your love deepen. This magical experience is perfect for couples who appreciate the beauty of nature.

6. Private Yacht Charter:

Indulge in the ultimate luxury by chartering a private yacht for a day or overnight excursion. Cruise the pristine waters, visit secluded coves, and enjoy gourmet meals prepared onboard. This exclusive experience will allow you and your partner to relax and enjoy each other's company in complete privacy.

7. Helicopter Tour:

Soar above the United States Virgin Islands on a thrilling helicopter tour. Witness the breathtaking beauty of the islands from a unique perspective and share the exhilaration with your significant other. This adventure will create an unforgettable memory that you can cherish together.

8. Sunset Dinner at a Fine Dining Restaurant:

Experience a romantic evening with a sunset dinner at one of the fine dining restaurants overlooking the ocean. Indulge in exquisite cuisine, sip on fine wines, and let the ambiance set the stage for an intimate and unforgettable evening.

9. Moonlit Beach Stroll:

Take a moonlit stroll along one of the many pristine beaches in the United States Virgin Islands. Let the soft sand tickle your toes as you hold hands and enjoy the tranquility of the night. This simple yet romantic activity allows you to connect with nature and each other.

10. Couples' Cooking Class:

Enroll in a couples' cooking class and learn to create delectable Caribbean dishes together. Explore the local flavors, sharpen your culinary skills, and bond over the art of cooking. This interactive and romantic experience will leave you with lasting memories and new recipes to recreate at home.

Conclusion:

The United States Virgin Islands offers a wide array of romantic activities for couples seeking a memorable getaway. From sunset cruises to private beach picnics, snorkeling adventures to moonlit beach strolls, these experiences will enhance your connection and create cherished moments with your loved one. Embrace the beauty of this Caribbean paradise and let the United States Virgin Islands become the backdrop for your own love story.

Chapter 27: Activities for Solo Travelers in United States Virgin Islands

Introduction:

Embarking on a solo journey to the United States Virgin Islands is an exhilarating experience that offers endless opportunities for self-discovery and exploration. From stunning beaches to vibrant culture, this tropical paradise is a haven for solo travelers seeking adventure, relaxation, and personal growth. In this chapter, we will unveil the top 10 activities that will make your solo trip to the United States Virgin Islands an unforgettable one.

1. Discover the Magic of St. John:

Start your solo adventure by exploring the captivating island of St. John. Hike through the lush trails of the Virgin Islands National Park, snorkel in the crystal-clear waters of Trunk Bay, or simply relax on the pristine beaches. St. John's untouched beauty will leave you in awe.

2. Dive into the Underwater World:

The United States Virgin Islands boast some of the most spectacular diving spots in the Caribbean. Sign up for a diving excursion and explore vibrant coral reefs, encounter sea turtles, and swim alongside tropical fish. The underwater world will mesmerize you with its beauty and tranquility.

3. Sail Away to the British Virgin Islands:

Hop aboard a day cruise to the nearby British Virgin Islands and experience the thrill of sailing solo. Discover hidden coves, snorkel in secluded bays, and indulge in the laid-back atmosphere of Jost Van Dyke or Virgin Gorda. This adventure will provide you with a unique perspective of the Caribbean.

4. Immerse Yourself in History at Fort Christian:

Take a step back in time by visiting Fort Christian in Charlotte Amalie, St. Thomas. This historic landmark, built in the 17th century, offers a glimpse into the island's past. Explore the exhibits, admire the architecture, and learn about the rich cultural heritage of the United States Virgin Islands.

5. Indulge in Island Cuisine:

No solo trip is complete without savoring the local flavors. Taste the unique blend of Caribbean and international cuisine at the vibrant food markets and beachside restaurants. From fresh seafood to mouthwatering jerk chicken, the United States Virgin Islands will tantalize your taste buds.

6. Capture the Perfect Sunset:

Witnessing a breathtaking sunset is a must-do for solo travelers. Head to Magens Bay Beach in St. Thomas or Caneel Bay in St. John and immerse yourself in the tranquility of the moment. As the sun dips below the horizon, you'll be reminded of the beauty and serenity of nature.

7. Explore Coral World Ocean Park:

For an up-close encounter with marine life, visit Coral World Ocean Park on St. Thomas. Dive into the underwater observatory and marvel at the colorful coral reefs, swim with sea lions, or feed the stingrays. This interactive experience will leave you with unforgettable memories.

8. Hike to the Top of Sage Mountain:

Challenge yourself by hiking to the summit of Sage Mountain, the highest point in the United States Virgin Islands. As you ascend through the lush rainforest, you'll be rewarded with breathtaking panoramic views of the surrounding islands. This solo adventure will invigorate your spirit and connect you with nature.

9. Shop for Local Treasures:

Explore the vibrant markets and boutiques of Charlotte Amalie, St. Thomas, and find unique souvenirs to remind you of your solo journey. From local artwork to handmade jewelry, the United States Virgin Islands offer a treasure trove of authentic Caribbean crafts.

10. Connect with the Locals:

Embrace the warm hospitality of the locals and engage in cultural activities. Attend a traditional music festival, participate in a cooking class, or join a local dance workshop. Interacting with the vibrant community will enrich your solo travel experience and create lasting memories.

Conclusion:

The United States Virgin Islands provide solo travelers with an abundance of activities that cater to every interest and passion. Whether you seek adventure, relaxation, or cultural immersion, these top 10 activities will ensure that your solo journey is one filled with exploration, personal growth, and unforgettable experiences. Embark on this tropical paradise and create memories that will last a lifetime.

Chapter 28: Budget-friendly activities in United States Virgin Islands

Introduction:

Welcome to the United States Virgin Islands, a tropical paradise in the Caribbean that offers a wide range of budget-friendly activities for every traveler. From breathtaking beaches to vibrant cultural experiences, this chapter will guide you through the top 10 affordable activities that will make your trip to the US Virgin Islands unforgettable without breaking the bank.

1. Explore the National Parks:

The US Virgin Islands is home to three stunning national parks: Virgin Islands National Park on St. John, Buck Island Reef National Monument on St. Croix, and Salt River Bay National Historical Park and Ecological Preserve on St. Croix. These parks offer free or low-cost admission, allowing you to immerse yourself in the islands' natural beauty through hiking, snorkeling, and wildlife spotting.

2. Relax on Budget-Friendly Beaches:

The US Virgin Islands boasts some of the most pristine beaches in the world. While some beaches may require an entrance fee, many public beaches are free to access. Pack a picnic, grab your beach towel, and spend a day sunbathing, swimming, and snorkeling at popular spots like Magens Bay on St. Thomas or Trunk Bay on St. John.

3. Visit Historic Sites:

Immerse yourself in the rich history of the US Virgin Islands by exploring its historic sites. Fort Christiansvaern on St. Croix and Fort Christian on St. Thomas are both open to the public and offer free or affordable admission. These well-preserved structures provide a glimpse into the islands' colonial past and offer stunning views of the surrounding areas.

4. Discover Local Markets:

Experience the vibrant local culture by visiting the bustling markets in the US Virgin Islands. The Market Square on St. Thomas and the Frederiksted Market on St. Croix are excellent places to find fresh produce, local crafts, and souvenirs at reasonable prices. Engage with the friendly locals, sample delicious Caribbean cuisine, and support the local economy.

5. Snorkel at Coral Reefs:

The US Virgin Islands is renowned for its breathtaking coral reefs, teeming with colorful marine life. While some snorkeling tours can be expensive, you can still enjoy this activity on a budget. Many beaches offer easy access to vibrant reefs, such as Coki Point on St. Thomas or Waterlemon Cay on St. John. Bring your snorkel gear or rent it at an affordable price and dive into the crystal-clear waters.

6. Hike the Virgin Islands' Trails:

For nature enthusiasts, the US Virgin Islands offers numerous hiking trails that showcase the islands' diverse landscapes. The Reef Bay Trail on St. John takes you through lush forests, past ancient petroglyphs, and ends at a picturesque beach. The Annaly Bay Tide Pools on St. Croix offer a unique hiking experience, leading you to natural tide pools where you can swim and relax.

7. Attend Local Festivals:

Immerse yourself in the vibrant local culture by attending one of the many festivals that take place throughout the year. The St. Thomas Carnival in April and the Crucian Christmas Festival in December are two of the most popular events. These festivals offer a range of affordable activities, including parades, local cuisine, live music, and traditional dance performances.

8. Visit the Virgin Islands Sustainable Farm Institute:

Located on St. Croix, the Virgin Islands Sustainable Farm Institute (VISFI) offers a unique and educational experience for budget-conscious travelers. Take a guided tour of the farm, learn about sustainable agriculture practices, and even participate in hands-on workshops. This eco-friendly attraction promotes environmental awareness and supports the local community.

9. Explore Historic Towns:

Take a stroll through the charming historic towns of Charlotte Amalie on St. Thomas and Christiansted on St. Croix. These towns are filled with colorful colonial architecture, quaint shops, and local restaurants. Enjoy window shopping, sample local delicacies, and soak in the authentic Caribbean atmosphere without spending a fortune.

10. Enjoy Free Local Entertainment:

Throughout the US Virgin Islands, you'll find various free or low-cost entertainment options. Check local event listings for live music performances, outdoor movie screenings, art exhibitions, and cultural shows. Many of these events are hosted at public parks or community centers, allowing you to experience the vibrant local scene without breaking your budget.

Conclusion:

The United States Virgin Islands offers a plethora of budget-friendly activities that allow you to explore its natural beauty, immerse yourself in the local culture, and create lasting memories without overspending. From national parks to stunning beaches, historic sites to vibrant festivals, there's something for every budget-conscious traveler in this tropical paradise. So pack your bags, plan your itinerary, and get ready for an affordable adventure in the US Virgin Islands.

Chapter 29: Off-the-beaten-path activities in United States Virgin Islands

Introduction:

Welcome to the United States Virgin Islands, a tropical paradise in the Caribbean known for its stunning beaches, crystal-clear waters, and vibrant culture. While the popular tourist attractions are undoubtedly breathtaking, there is a hidden side to these islands that is waiting to be explored. In this chapter, we will uncover the top 10 off-the-beaten-path activities that will take you on an unforgettable journey through the lesser-known gems of the United States Virgin Islands.

1. Hike to the Annaly Bay Tide Pools:

Escape the crowds and embark on a scenic hike to the Annaly Bay Tide Pools on St. Croix. This hidden oasis offers a unique opportunity to swim in natural saltwater pools while surrounded by dramatic cliffs and lush vegetation. The hike itself is an adventure, rewarding you with stunning panoramic views of the Caribbean Sea.

2. Discover the Ruins of the Annaberg Sugar Plantation:

Step back in time and explore the ruins of the Annaberg Sugar Plantation on St. John. This historical site provides a glimpse into the island's colonial past, with crumbling stone walls, windmill ruins, and interpretive signs that tell the story of the island's once-thriving sugar industry. Take a self-guided tour and immerse yourself in the rich history of the Virgin Islands.

3. Snorkel at Waterlemon Cay:

Escape the crowds and head to the secluded Waterlemon Cay on St. John. This off-the-beaten-path snorkeling spot offers crystal-clear waters teeming with vibrant marine life, including colorful coral reefs, tropical fish, and even the occasional sea turtle. Pack your snorkel gear and prepare for an unforgettable underwater adventure.

4. Explore the Salt River Bay National Historical Park:

Venture off the beaten path on St. Croix and visit the Salt River Bay National Historical Park. This hidden gem is home to a protected marine ecosystem, ancient archaeological sites, and a rich history that dates back over a thousand years. Take a kayak tour through the mangroves, visit the Amerindian archaeological sites, and learn about the area's significance in the history of the Virgin Islands.

5. Visit the Coral World Ocean Park:

Located on St. Thomas, the Coral World Ocean Park offers a unique opportunity to get up close and personal with marine life. Take a guided tour of the park's underwater observatory, walk through the vibrant coral reef tank, and even swim with sea lions or sharks. This off-the-beaten-path attraction provides an educational and interactive experience for visitors of all ages.

6. Kayak through the Bioluminescent Bay:

Embark on a magical journey through the bioluminescent bay on St. Croix. As night falls, the waters come alive with millions of tiny organisms that emit a mesmerizing glow. Paddle through the darkness and witness nature's own light show, creating a truly unforgettable experience.

7. Explore the Petroglyphs at Reef Bay:

Discover the ancient petroglyphs hidden within the lush rainforest of St. John's Reef Bay. Hike through the scenic trail, guided by interpretive signs that explain the history and significance of these prehistoric rock carvings. Immerse yourself in the island's rich cultural heritage and connect with the past.

8. Go Off-Roading on St. Thomas:

Leave the beaten path behind and embark on an off-roading adventure on St. Thomas. Rent a 4x4 vehicle and explore the island's hidden treasures, from secluded beaches to breathtaking viewpoints. Discover the true beauty of the island as you navigate through rugged terrain and immerse yourself in nature.

9. Visit the Virgin Islands Sustainable Farm Institute:

Escape the touristy areas and visit the Virgin Islands Sustainable Farm Institute on St. Croix. This organic farm offers guided tours that provide insight into sustainable agriculture, permaculture, and the importance of local food production. Learn about the island's efforts towards sustainability and enjoy fresh, farm-to-table meals made from locally sourced ingredients.

10. Dive the Wrecks of the Virgin Islands:

For adventure seekers, diving the wrecks of the Virgin Islands is an experience not to be missed. Explore the underwater world and discover sunken ships, planes, and artificial reefs that have become havens for marine life. With numerous dive sites scattered throughout the islands, you can choose from a variety of wrecks suitable for all skill levels.

Conclusion:

The United States Virgin Islands offer more than just sun, sand, and sea. By venturing off the beaten path, you can uncover hidden treasures, immerse yourself in the rich history and culture, and create unforgettable memories. From hiking to hidden tide pools to exploring ancient ruins, these off-the-beaten-path activities will allow you to truly experience the unique charm of the United States Virgin Islands.

Chapter 30: Sustainable Tourism Experiences in United States Virgin Islands

Introduction:

The United States Virgin Islands (USVI) is not only a tropical paradise but also a leading destination for sustainable tourism experiences. With its commitment to preserving the natural environment and promoting responsible tourism practices, the USVI offers a range of unique and eco-friendly activities for visitors to enjoy. In this chapter, we will explore the top 10 sustainable tourism experiences that showcase the USVI's dedication to sustainability and provide travelers with unforgettable memories.

1. Coral Reef Conservation:

The USVI is home to some of the most beautiful coral reefs in the world. Dive or snorkel in designated marine parks, such as Buck Island Reef National Monument, and witness the vibrant marine life while learning about coral reef conservation efforts. Participate in organized beach cleanups and contribute to the preservation of these delicate ecosystems.

2. Sustainable Farm Tours:

Embark on a guided tour of organic farms in St. Croix and St. Thomas. Learn about sustainable agriculture practices, sample fresh produce, and support local farmers who prioritize environmentally friendly methods. Discover the importance of sustainable food systems and the role they play in reducing carbon footprints.

3. Eco-Friendly Accommodations:

Choose from a variety of eco-friendly accommodations that have implemented sustainable practices. From solar-powered resorts to hotels with water conservation initiatives, these establishments prioritize environmental responsibility without compromising on comfort. Experience guilt-free luxury while minimizing your impact on the environment.

4. Hiking and Nature Trails:

Explore the USVI's lush landscapes through its extensive network of hiking and nature trails. Wander through the Virgin Islands National Park on St. John, where you can marvel at breathtaking views, spot endemic wildlife, and learn about the preservation efforts that protect the island's natural beauty.

5. Kayaking in Bioluminescent Bays:

Discover the magic of bioluminescence by kayaking through the glowing waters of the USVI's bioluminescent bays. These natural wonders are home to microscopic organisms that emit a mesmerizing blue-green light. Opt for guided tours that prioritize responsible practices to protect these delicate ecosystems.

6. Sustainable Fishing Charters:

Experience sustainable fishing practices firsthand by joining a responsible fishing charter. Learn about catch-and-release techniques, support local fishermen who adhere to sustainable fishing regulations, and gain a deeper appreciation for the importance of preserving marine biodiversity.

7. Cultural Immersion:

Engage with the local culture and support sustainable community initiatives. Attend cultural festivals, visit local artisans, and contribute to the preservation of traditional crafts. By participating in these activities, you not only support the local economy but also help foster the continuation of cultural heritage.

8. Renewable Energy Initiatives:

Explore the USVI's commitment to renewable energy by visiting solar farms and wind turbine installations. Learn about the islands' transition to cleaner energy sources and witness the positive impact these initiatives have on reducing carbon emissions.

9. Volunteer Opportunities:

Engage in volunteer programs that focus on environmental conservation and sustainable development. Join local organizations in beach cleanups, reforestation projects, or educational programs that promote environmental awareness. Make a meaningful contribution to the USVI's sustainability efforts.

10. Responsible Water Sports:

Participate in water sports activities, such as paddleboarding and kayaking, with operators who prioritize responsible practices. Choose companies that adhere to guidelines for wildlife protection and educate visitors about the importance of responsible interactions with marine life.

Conclusion:

The United States Virgin Islands is not only a tropical paradise but also a shining example of sustainable tourism practices. By offering a wide range of eco-friendly experiences, the USVI ensures that visitors can enjoy its natural beauty while contributing to its preservation. From coral reef conservation to cultural immersion, there are countless ways to make a positive impact and create unforgettable memories in this sustainable haven.

Chapter 31: Responsible Tourism Experiences in United States Virgin Islands

Introduction:

Welcome to the stunning United States Virgin Islands (USVI), a tropical paradise in the Caribbean known for its pristine beaches, vibrant culture, and rich history. In this chapter, we will explore the top 10 responsible tourism experiences that allow visitors to appreciate the natural beauty of the islands while supporting sustainable practices and local communities.

1. Coral Reef Conservation:

Embark on a snorkeling or diving adventure to witness the breathtaking coral reefs surrounding the USVI. Join a responsible tour operator that educates visitors about the importance of preserving these delicate ecosystems. Learn how to protect and conserve coral reefs, and contribute to ongoing research efforts aimed at their preservation.

2. Sustainable Farm Visits:

Discover the sustainable farming practices that are revolutionizing the local food scene in the USVI. Visit organic farms and learn about their innovative techniques, such as aquaponics and permaculture. Engage in farm-to-table experiences where you can savor fresh, locally grown produce and support the local economy.

3. Kayaking through Mangrove Forests:

Explore the enchanting mangrove forests of the USVI by kayaking through their narrow channels. Choose a responsible tour operator that emphasizes the importance of preserving these vital coastal ecosystems. Learn about the unique flora and fauna that call the mangroves home, and understand the role they play in protecting the islands from erosion and storm damage.

4. Volunteering at Wildlife Rehabilitation Centers:

Make a positive impact on the local wildlife by volunteering at wildlife rehabilitation centers in the USVI. Assist in the care and rehabilitation of injured or orphaned animals, such as sea turtles and birds. Gain a deeper understanding of the challenges faced by these species and contribute to their conservation efforts.

5. Cultural Immersion in Local Communities:

Immerse yourself in the vibrant culture of the USVI by engaging with local communities. Participate in responsible cultural tours that introduce you to traditional music, dance, and cuisine. Support local artisans by purchasing handmade crafts and learn about their cultural significance.

6. Sustainable Sailing and Yachting:

Experience the beauty of the USVI from the water by engaging in responsible sailing and yachting activities. Choose operators that prioritize sustainable practices, such as using eco-friendly fuels and minimizing waste. Explore secluded coves, pristine beaches, and protected marine areas while leaving minimal impact on the environment.

7. Eco-friendly Accommodations:

Opt for eco-friendly accommodations during your stay in the USVI. Choose hotels and resorts that have implemented sustainable practices, such as energy and water conservation, waste management, and supporting local communities. By staying in these establishments, you directly contribute to responsible tourism initiatives.

8. Hiking and Nature Trails:

Embark on hiking and nature trails across the USVI to immerse yourself in the natural beauty of the islands. Choose responsible tour operators that promote Leave No Trace principles and educate visitors about the importance of preserving the fragile ecosystems. Learn about the unique flora and fauna while enjoying breathtaking views.

9. Supporting Local Conservation Organizations:

Support local conservation organizations in the USVI by donating or participating in their initiatives. These organizations work tirelessly to protect the islands' natural resources and wildlife. By contributing, you actively participate in responsible tourism and help ensure the preservation of the USVI's natural wonders for future generations.

10. Responsible Water Sports:

Engage in responsible water sports activities, such as paddleboarding, kayaking, and sailing, in the USVI. Choose operators that prioritize safety, environmental conservation, and education. Learn about the marine life and ecosystems you encounter, and understand how to minimize your impact on these fragile environments.

Conclusion:

The United States Virgin Islands offers a plethora of responsible tourism experiences that allow visitors to appreciate the natural wonders while supporting sustainable practices and local communities. By choosing responsible operators, engaging in educational activities, and supporting conservation efforts, you can make a positive impact and help preserve the beauty of the USVI for generations to come.

Chapter 32: Volunteer Opportunities in United States Virgin Islands

Introduction:

The United States Virgin Islands, with its stunning beaches, crystal-clear waters, and vibrant culture, is not only a popular tourist destination but also a place where visitors can make a positive impact through volunteering. In this chapter, we will explore the top ten volunteer opportunities available in the US Virgin Islands, allowing travelers to immerse themselves in the local community and contribute to its development.

1. Coral Reef Conservation:

The US Virgin Islands boast some of the most beautiful coral reefs in the world. Volunteers can join organizations such as The Nature Conservancy to help protect and restore these fragile ecosystems. Activities may include underwater cleanups, monitoring coral health, and educating visitors about sustainable practices.

2. Marine Wildlife Rehabilitation:

For animal lovers, volunteering at the St. Croix Environmental Association's marine wildlife rehabilitation center is an excellent opportunity. Assist in the rescue, rehabilitation, and release of injured sea turtles, dolphins, and other marine animals, while learning about their conservation needs.

3. National Park Maintenance:

The US Virgin Islands are home to three stunning national parks: Virgin Islands National Park, Buck Island Reef National Monument, and Christiansted National Historic Site. Volunteers can join park rangers in maintaining trails, restoring historic sites, and educating visitors about the importance of preserving these natural and cultural treasures.

4. Youth Mentorship Programs:

Many local organizations focus on empowering the youth of the US Virgin Islands. By volunteering with programs like the Boys and Girls Clubs or the Virgin Islands Youth Advocacy Coalition, you can make a positive impact on young lives through mentoring, tutoring, and organizing recreational activities.

5. Environmental Education:

Organizations like the Virgin Islands Conservation Society offer volunteer opportunities to educate local communities and tourists about the importance of environmental conservation. Assist in organizing workshops, beach cleanups, and awareness campaigns to promote sustainable practices and protect the islands' natural resources.

6. Community Development:

Volunteers can participate in community development projects, working alongside organizations like the Community Foundation of the Virgin Islands. Help rebuild homes, improve infrastructure, or support local entrepreneurs, contributing to the long-term growth and resilience of the islands' communities.

7. Animal Shelter Assistance:

Animal shelters in the US Virgin Islands often face challenges due to limited resources. By volunteering at organizations like the St. Thomas Humane Society, you can help care for abandoned or stray animals, assist with adoption events, and promote responsible pet ownership.

8. Elderly Care:

Volunteer programs like the St. John Community Foundation's Senior Connections provide opportunities to engage with the elderly population. Offer companionship, assist with daily activities, and organize social events to enhance the quality of life for senior citizens in the US Virgin Islands.

9. Sustainable Agriculture:

The US Virgin Islands are embracing sustainable farming practices to reduce their dependence on imported goods. Volunteers can join initiatives like the Virgin Islands Sustainable Farm Institute to learn about organic farming, help with crop cultivation, and support local food security efforts.

10. Disaster Preparedness and Relief:

Given the region's vulnerability to hurricanes and other natural disasters, volunteering with organizations like the Virgin Islands Voluntary Organizations Active in Disaster (VI VOAD) can be crucial. Assist in disaster preparedness campaigns, emergency response efforts, and recovery projects to help the islands bounce back stronger after a crisis.

Conclusion:

Volunteering in the United States Virgin Islands provides a unique opportunity to give back while experiencing the beauty of the Caribbean. By engaging in any of these top ten volunteer opportunities, you can make a lasting impact on the local community, preserve the islands' natural wonders, and create unforgettable memories of your time in this tropical paradise.

Chapter 33: Visas and Immigration Requirements for United States Virgin Islands

Introduction:

The United States Virgin Islands, a tropical paradise in the Caribbean, offers visitors a unique blend of American and Caribbean cultures. As a territory of the United States, the islands have specific visa and immigration requirements that travelers must adhere to. This chapter aims to provide a comprehensive overview of the visa and immigration regulations for those planning a visit to the United States Virgin Islands.

1. Visa-Free Entry:

The United States Virgin Islands allows visa-free entry for citizens of the United States, including U.S. nationals and U.S. permanent residents. Additionally, citizens of certain countries participating in the Visa Waiver Program (VWP) are also eligible for visa-free entry, provided they hold a valid Electronic System for Travel Authorization (ESTA).

2. Non-U.S. Citizens:

For non-U.S. citizens who are not eligible for visa-free entry, a valid U.S. visa is required to enter the United States Virgin Islands. It is important to note that the visa requirements for the United States Virgin Islands are the same as those for the mainland United States. Therefore, travelers should consult the U.S. Department of State or their nearest U.S. embassy or consulate for specific visa information.

3. Immigration Procedures:

Upon arrival in the United States Virgin Islands, all visitors, regardless of their citizenship, must go through U.S. immigration procedures. This includes presenting a valid passport and completing the necessary immigration forms. Visitors should be prepared to answer questions regarding the purpose of their visit, duration of stay, and address of accommodation.

4. Length of Stay:

Visitors to the United States Virgin Islands are generally granted a 90-day stay. However, it is important to note that this period is subject to the discretion of the U.S. Customs and Border Protection officer at the port of entry. If visitors wish to extend their stay beyond the initial 90 days, they must apply for an extension with the U.S. Citizenship and Immigration Services.

5. Work and Study Permits:

Foreign nationals who intend to work or study in the United States Virgin Islands must obtain the appropriate permits. Work permits, also known as employment authorization documents, are issued by the U.S. Citizenship and Immigration Services. Similarly, students planning to pursue education on the islands must obtain the necessary student visas, such as the F-1 visa for academic studies.

6. Permanent Residency and Citizenship:

For those interested in obtaining permanent residency or citizenship in the United States Virgin Islands, the process follows the same guidelines as applying for these statuses in the mainland United States. It is advisable to seek legal counsel or consult the U.S. Department of Homeland Security for detailed information on eligibility criteria and application procedures.

Conclusion:

Understanding the visa and immigration requirements for the United States Virgin Islands is crucial for a smooth and enjoyable visit. This chapter has provided a comprehensive overview of the regulations, emphasizing the importance of adhering to the guidelines set by the U.S. government. By familiarizing yourself with these requirements, you can embark on your journey to the United States Virgin Islands with confidence and peace of mind.

Chapter 34: Money and Banking in United States Virgin Islands

Introduction:

Welcome to the United States Virgin Islands! As you embark on your journey, it is essential to familiarize yourself with the local currency, exchange rates, ATMs, and credit card usage. This chapter will provide you with all the necessary information to ensure a smooth and convenient financial experience during your visit to this stunning Caribbean destination.

Currency:

The official currency of the United States Virgin Islands is the United States Dollar (USD). The currency is widely accepted throughout the islands, making it convenient for tourists to conduct transactions without the need for currency exchange.

Exchange Rates:

As the United States Dollar is the official currency, there is no need to worry about fluctuating exchange rates. However, it's always advisable to stay informed about the current exchange rates between your local currency and the USD to have a better understanding of the value of your money.

ATMs:

ATMs are readily available across the United States Virgin Islands, making it easy to access cash when needed. Most ATMs accept major international debit and credit cards. However, it is recommended to inform your bank about your travel plans to avoid any potential issues with card usage.

While withdrawing cash from ATMs, it's important to be aware of any associated fees. Some ATMs may charge a nominal fee for international transactions, so it's advisable to withdraw larger amounts to minimize the frequency of withdrawals and associated fees.

Credit Cards:

Credit cards are widely accepted in the United States Virgin Islands. Most establishments, including hotels, restaurants, and shops, readily accept major credit cards such as Visa, MasterCard, and American Express. However, it's always a good idea to carry some cash for smaller establishments or places that might not accept cards.

Before using your credit card, it is recommended to notify your bank about your travel plans to avoid any potential issues with card authorization. Additionally, be cautious when using your card for online transactions or in unfamiliar establishments to protect yourself from potential fraud.

Safety Measures:

While the United States Virgin Islands is a safe destination for tourists, it is always advisable to practice caution when handling money. Keep an eye on your belongings, especially in crowded areas, and avoid displaying large sums of cash in public. It's also recommended to store your cash, cards, and important documents in a secure place, such as a hotel safe, to minimize the risk of loss or theft.

Conclusion:

Understanding the currency, exchange rates, ATM availability, and credit card usage in the United States Virgin Islands is crucial for a hassle-free and convenient experience during your visit. By following the tips and information provided in this chapter, you can confidently navigate the local banking system and enjoy a worry-free financial journey in this breathtaking Caribbean paradise.

Chapter 35: Communication in United States Virgin Islands

Introduction:

Welcome to Chapter 35 of our tourist guide, where we will explore the communication infrastructure in the United States Virgin Islands. In this chapter, we will provide you with a summary of the phone system, internet access, and postal service available in this beautiful Caribbean destination.

1. The Phone System:

The United States Virgin Islands boasts a reliable and efficient phone system that allows both locals and visitors to stay connected. The country's telephone network is modern and well-maintained, ensuring clear and uninterrupted communication. Most hotels, resorts, and businesses provide direct dialing services, allowing visitors to make local and international calls easily. It is important to note that international calls may incur additional charges, so it is recommended to inquire about rates before making long-distance calls.

2. Internet Access:

Staying connected while exploring the United States Virgin Islands is a breeze, thanks to the widespread availability of internet access. Most hotels, resorts, and cafes offer free Wi-Fi for their guests, allowing you to stay connected and share your experiences with friends and family back home. Additionally, the country has several internet cafes where visitors can access the internet for a small fee. Whether you need to check your emails, browse the web, or share your vacation photos on social media, you'll find reliable internet access throughout the islands.

3. Postal Service:

The United States Virgin Islands has a well-established postal service that ensures efficient mail delivery both domestically and internationally. The local post offices are conveniently located in various towns and cities, making it easy for visitors to send postcards, letters, or packages back home. The postal service offers a range of mailing options, including express delivery for urgent items. It is important to note that postage rates may vary depending on the destination, size, and weight of the item being sent. Visitors are advised to inquire about these rates at the post office or consult the official postal service website for accurate information.

Conclusion:

In conclusion, the United States Virgin Islands provides visitors with excellent communication infrastructure, ensuring that you can stay connected throughout your stay. The phone system is reliable and allows for easy local and international calls, while internet access is widely available, allowing you to stay connected online. The postal service ensures efficient mail delivery, allowing you to send postcards and packages back home with ease. As you explore this beautiful Caribbean destination, rest assured that you will have no trouble staying connected and communicating with your loved ones.

Chapter 36: Health and Safety in United States Virgin Islands

Introduction:

As you embark on your journey to the beautiful United States Virgin Islands, it is important to prioritize your health and safety. This chapter provides a comprehensive overview of common health risks and essential safety tips to ensure a worry-free and enjoyable experience. Please note that while the islands offer a generally safe environment, it is always advisable to exercise caution and take necessary precautions.

1. Medical Facilities and Services:

The United States Virgin Islands boast modern medical facilities and services. The main hospital, Roy Lester Schneider Hospital, is located on St. Thomas and provides quality healthcare. Additionally, there are numerous private clinics and pharmacies throughout the islands. It is recommended to have comprehensive travel insurance that covers medical expenses and emergency evacuation.

2. Vaccinations and Health Precautions:

Before traveling to the United States Virgin Islands, it is advisable to consult your healthcare provider regarding necessary vaccinations. Routine vaccinations such as measles-mumps-rubella (MMR), diphtheria-tetanus-pertussis, and influenza are recommended. Hepatitis A and B vaccines are also recommended for most travelers. It is crucial to practice good hygiene, including frequent handwashing, to minimize the risk of common illnesses.

3. Mosquito-Borne Diseases:

The United States Virgin Islands have reported cases of mosquito-borne diseases, including dengue fever and Zika virus. To prevent mosquito bites, use insect repellents containing DEET, wear long-sleeved clothing, and utilize bed nets if necessary. It is also advisable to avoid stagnant water and remove any potential breeding sites around your accommodation.

4. Sun Safety:

With its stunning beaches and tropical climate, sun safety is paramount in the United States Virgin Islands. Protect yourself from harmful UV rays by wearing sunscreen with a high SPF, seeking shade during peak hours, and wearing protective clothing, such as hats and sunglasses. Stay hydrated and be mindful of heat-related illnesses by drinking plenty of water and taking breaks in air-conditioned areas.

5. Water Safety:

While the United States Virgin Islands offer crystal-clear waters, it is important to be cautious when swimming or engaging in water activities. Always swim in designated areas with lifeguards present. Be aware of strong currents and undertows, especially during rough weather conditions. It is advisable to follow safety guidelines and heed any warnings issued by local authorities.

6. Food and Water Hygiene:

To avoid gastrointestinal illnesses, practice good food and water hygiene. Drink bottled water or boil tap water before consumption. Ensure that food is thoroughly cooked and served hot. Avoid consuming raw or undercooked seafood, as well as street food from unverified vendors. Additionally, wash your hands before eating and use hand sanitizers when necessary.

7. Crime Prevention:

While the United States Virgin Islands are generally safe, it is essential to take precautions to prevent any potential crimes. Avoid displaying valuable items and keep your belongings secure at all times. Use reputable transportation services and avoid walking alone in secluded areas, particularly at night. Stay informed about your surroundings and report any suspicious activities to local authorities.

Conclusion:

By prioritizing your health and safety, you can fully enjoy the wonders of the United States Virgin Islands. Remember to consult with healthcare professionals, take necessary vaccinations, and practice good hygiene. Be mindful of potential risks such as mosquito-borne diseases, sun exposure, and water safety. By following these guidelines, you can have a memorable and worry-free experience in this tropical paradise.

Chapter 37: Travel Insurance for United States Virgin Islands

Introduction:

As you embark on your journey to the breathtaking United States Virgin Islands, it is essential to prioritize your safety and well-being. While planning an unforgettable vacation, it is crucial to consider unforeseen circumstances that may disrupt your travel plans. In this chapter, we will explore the benefits of travel insurance and guide you on how to purchase the right coverage for your trip to the United States Virgin Islands.

Understanding the Benefits of Travel Insurance:

1. Trip Cancellation or Interruption Coverage:

Travel insurance provides financial protection in case you need to cancel or cut short your trip due to unforeseen events such as illness, injury, or natural disasters. This coverage ensures that you can recover your non-refundable expenses, allowing you to rebook your vacation at a later time without incurring additional costs.

2. Emergency Medical Expenses:

While in the United States Virgin Islands, it is essential to have adequate medical coverage in case of unexpected illnesses or accidents. Travel insurance can cover medical expenses, including hospital stays, emergency medical evacuation, and repatriation of remains, ensuring you receive the necessary care without worrying about the financial burden.

3. Baggage and Personal Belongings:

Losing your luggage or having your personal belongings stolen can be distressing. Travel insurance offers coverage for lost, stolen, or damaged baggage, as well as personal belongings such as cameras, laptops, and jewelry. This coverage ensures that you can replace your items and continue enjoying your vacation without any inconvenience.

4. Travel Delay or Missed Connection:

Flight delays and missed connections can disrupt your travel plans and result in additional expenses. With travel insurance, you can receive compensation for additional accommodation, meals, and transportation costs incurred due to travel delays. This coverage provides peace of mind and allows you to make the most of your time in the United States Virgin Islands.

Purchasing Travel Insurance:

1. Assess Your Needs:

Before purchasing travel insurance, carefully evaluate your travel plans, medical needs, and personal belongings. Consider factors such as trip duration, activities you plan to engage in, and the value of your belongings to determine the coverage that suits you best.

2. Research and Compare:

To ensure you find the most suitable travel insurance for your trip to the United States Virgin Islands, research and compare different insurance providers. Look for reputable companies that offer comprehensive coverage at competitive prices. Read reviews and seek recommendations from fellow travelers to make an informed decision.

3. Read the Policy Details:

Before finalizing your purchase, carefully read the policy details to understand the coverage, exclusions, and claim procedures. Pay attention to specific terms and conditions that may affect your coverage, such as pre-existing medical conditions or high-value items.

4. Purchase in Advance:

It is advisable to purchase travel insurance as soon as you book your trip to the United States Virgin Islands. By doing so, you can benefit from coverage for trip cancellation or interruption due to unforeseen events that may occur before your departure.

Conclusion:

Travel insurance is an essential investment when planning your trip to the United States Virgin Islands. By understanding the benefits and purchasing the right coverage, you can protect yourself from unexpected expenses and enjoy a worry-free vacation. Remember to choose a reputable insurance provider, assess your needs, and carefully read the policy details to ensure you have the necessary protection throughout your journey.

Chapter 38: Learning the Language of United States Virgin Islands

Introduction:

Welcome to Chapter 38 of our comprehensive tourist guide on the United States Virgin Islands. In this chapter, we will explore the unique language spoken in this beautiful Caribbean destination. Learning the local language can greatly enhance your travel experience, allowing you to connect with the culture and people on a deeper level. We will provide you with a summary of the resources available for learning the language of the United States Virgin Islands, ensuring that your linguistic journey is both truthful and authentic.

1. The Language of the United States Virgin Islands:

The United States Virgin Islands is a melting pot of cultures, resulting in a diverse linguistic landscape. The official language is English, as the islands are a territory of the United States. However, you will also encounter a Creole language known as Virgin Islands Creole English (V.I. Creole) spoken by many locals.

2. Learning English:

For travelers seeking to improve their English skills, the United States Virgin Islands offers a range of resources. Whether you are a beginner or an advanced learner, you can find language schools, private tutors, and online platforms that cater to your specific needs. These resources provide comprehensive English language courses, focusing on grammar, vocabulary, pronunciation, and conversation skills.

3. Discovering Virgin Islands Creole English:

To truly immerse yourself in the local culture, learning a few phrases in Virgin Islands Creole English can be immensely rewarding. This unique Creole language is a blend of English, African languages, and other Caribbean influences. While not necessary for basic communication, knowing a few key phrases can enhance your interactions and demonstrate your respect for the local culture.

4. Local Language Resources:

To learn Virgin Islands Creole English, you can take advantage of various resources. Local language schools and cultural centers offer courses specifically tailored to teach you the basics of the language.

Additionally, you can find books, audio materials, and online resources that provide insights into the grammar, vocabulary, and pronunciation of Virgin Islands Creole English.

5. Language Exchange Opportunities:

Engaging in language exchange programs can be a fantastic way to practice your language skills and connect with locals. Many language schools and community organizations organize language exchange events, where you can meet native speakers and practice both English and Virgin Islands Creole English. These interactions will not only improve your language abilities but also allow you to forge meaningful connections with the local community.

Conclusion:

Learning the language of the United States Virgin Islands can enrich your travel experience and foster a deeper understanding of the local culture. Whether you choose to focus on improving your English or venture into learning Virgin Islands Creole English, the resources available on the islands will cater to your needs. Embrace the opportunity to communicate with locals in their native tongue, and you will undoubtedly create unforgettable memories during your time in the United States Virgin Islands.

Chapter 39: Tips for Traveling with Children in United States Virgin Islands

Traveling with children can be an exciting and memorable experience, especially when visiting the beautiful United States Virgin Islands. With its stunning beaches, rich history, and family-friendly attractions, the USVI offers a fantastic destination for families. To ensure a smooth and enjoyable trip, here are some valuable tips to consider when traveling with children in the United States Virgin Islands.

1. Pack Smartly:

When traveling with children, packing efficiently is essential. Make sure to pack plenty of sunscreen, hats, and protective clothing to shield your little ones from the sun's rays. Additionally, packing insect repellent is crucial, as mosquitoes can be prevalent in some areas. Don't forget to bring any necessary medications, baby supplies, and a first aid kit for any unforeseen circumstances.

2. Choose Family-Friendly Accommodations:

When selecting accommodations, opt for family-friendly resorts or hotels that offer amenities specifically designed for children. Look for properties with kid's clubs, playgrounds, and swimming pools, as these facilities can provide additional entertainment and relaxation opportunities for your little ones.

3. Plan Outdoor Activities:

The United States Virgin Islands offer an array of outdoor activities that are perfect for families. Consider planning activities such as snorkeling, sailing, or kayaking, as these allow children to explore the stunning marine life and crystal-clear waters. Remember to check the age restrictions and safety measures for each activity to ensure the suitability for your children.

4. Visit Family-Oriented Attractions:

The USVI boasts numerous attractions that cater to families. Take your children to explore the Coral World Ocean Park, where they can marvel at the underwater wonders through an underwater observatory or swim with sea lions. The Butterfly Garden and Botanical Garden of St. Thomas are also excellent choices for a day filled with educational and interactive experiences. Don't miss the chance to visit the St. Thomas Skyride, where your family can enjoy breathtaking views of the islands from above.

5. Embrace the Local Culture:

Immerse your children in the rich history and culture of the United States Virgin Islands. Visit historical sites such as Fort Christian in Charlotte Amalie or the Annaberg Sugar Plantation Ruins on St. John, where they can learn about the islands' past. Encourage them to try local cuisine, such as johnnycakes or conch fritters, to experience the authentic flavors of the Caribbean.

6. Be Mindful of Safety:

While the USVI is generally a safe destination, it's crucial to remain vigilant, especially when traveling with children. Keep a close eye on your little ones at all times, particularly in crowded areas or near water. Teach them about water safety and ensure they wear life jackets when participating in water activities. Familiarize yourself with emergency contact numbers and the location of nearby medical facilities, just in case.

7. Respect the Environment:

Encourage your children to be responsible travelers by respecting the environment. Teach them about the importance of preserving the natural beauty of the islands, such as not littering and avoiding touching or disturbing wildlife. Participate in local beach clean-ups or conservation activities to instill a sense of environmental stewardship in your children.

Traveling with children in the United States Virgin Islands can create lasting memories for the whole family. By following these tips, you can ensure a safe, enjoyable, and unforgettable experience that will leave your children longing to return to this tropical paradise.

Chapter 40: Tips for Traveling with Seniors in the United States Virgin Islands

Introduction:

Traveling with seniors can be a rewarding and memorable experience, especially when visiting the beautiful United States Virgin Islands. With its stunning beaches, rich history, and vibrant culture, this tropical paradise offers countless opportunities for seniors to relax, explore, and create lasting memories. To ensure a smooth and enjoyable trip, here are some essential tips on what to pack, where to stay, and things to do when traveling with seniors in the United States Virgin Islands.

What to Pack:

1. Medications: It is crucial to pack an ample supply of prescription medications, along with a list of emergency contacts and medical information. Consider carrying a small first aid kit for minor injuries or ailments.

2. Comfortable Clothing: Pack lightweight and breathable clothing suitable for the tropical climate. Don't forget to include comfortable walking shoes for exploring the island's attractions.

3. Sun Protection: The Caribbean sun can be intense, so bring wide-brimmed hats, sunglasses, and sunscreen with a high SPF to protect against harmful UV rays.

4. Travel Documents: Ensure all necessary travel documents, such as passports, identification, and travel insurance, are safely packed and easily accessible.

5. Snacks and Water: Keep a supply of snacks and bottled water handy to stay hydrated and energized during excursions.

Where to Stay:

1. Accessibility: When choosing accommodation, opt for hotels or resorts that offer accessible rooms or have facilities catering to seniors with mobility challenges.

2. Proximity to Amenities: Select accommodations that are conveniently located near restaurants, shops, and medical facilities to ensure easy access to essential services.

3. Safety and Security: Prioritize accommodations with adequate security measures, such as well-lit pathways and 24-hour security, to ensure a safe and worry-free stay.

4. Comfort and Relaxation: Look for hotels or resorts that offer amenities like spa services, comfortable lounges, or scenic views, allowing seniors to unwind and enjoy their vacation to the fullest.

Things to Do:

1. Beaches: The United States Virgin Islands boast some of the most breathtaking beaches in the Caribbean. Encourage seniors to relax on the soft sand, take a dip in the crystal-clear waters, or simply enjoy the tranquil surroundings.

2. Historical Sites: Explore the rich history of the islands by visiting historical landmarks such as Blackbeard's Castle, Fort Christian, or the Annaberg Sugar Plantation. Many sites offer guided tours and have accessible pathways for seniors.

3. Nature Excursions: Embark on scenic nature excursions, such as eco-tours or boat trips to the nearby islands. Seniors can marvel at the stunning coral reefs, go birdwatching, or even take a leisurely hike through the lush rainforests.

4. Cultural Experiences: Immerse yourselves in the vibrant local culture by attending cultural festivals, visiting art galleries, or enjoying live music performances. Seniors can also savor the local cuisine and indulge in traditional dishes.

5. Relaxation Activities: Encourage seniors to pamper themselves with spa treatments, yoga classes, or leisurely walks in botanical

gardens. These activities offer a chance to unwind and rejuvenate amidst the island's natural beauty.

Conclusion:

Traveling with seniors to the United States Virgin Islands can be an unforgettable experience filled with relaxation, exploration, and cultural enrichment. By following these tips on what to pack, where to stay, and things to do, you can ensure a smooth and enjoyable trip for both yourself and your senior companions. Remember to prioritize their comfort, safety, and accessibility, allowing them to fully embrace the beauty and charm of this tropical paradise.

Chapter 41: Tips for Traveling Solo in the United States Virgin Islands

Introduction:

Traveling solo can be an incredibly liberating and rewarding experience, especially in the stunning United States Virgin Islands. With its breathtaking beaches, vibrant culture, and friendly locals, this tropical paradise is an ideal destination for solo travelers seeking both relaxation and adventure. In this chapter, we will provide you with valuable tips on where to stay, things to do, and how to stay safe during your solo journey in the United States Virgin Islands.

Where to Stay:

1. Choose a Safe and Convenient Location: When traveling solo, it's important to select accommodation in a safe and well-connected area. St. Thomas and St. John are popular islands offering a range of accommodations, from luxury resorts to budget-friendly guesthouses. Consider staying in areas such as Charlotte Amalie or Cruz Bay, which have a good selection of hotels, restaurants, and amenities.

2. Opt for Social Accommodations: If you're looking to meet fellow travelers and make new friends, consider staying in hostels or guesthouses that offer communal spaces. These accommodations often organize group activities or have common areas where you can socialize and connect with other solo travelers.

Things to Do:

1. Explore the Pristine Beaches: The United States Virgin Islands are renowned for their stunning beaches, so make sure to spend ample time soaking up the sun and enjoying the crystal-clear waters. Popular beaches include Magens Bay in St. Thomas, Trunk Bay in St. John, and Cane Garden Bay in Tortola. Remember to bring sunscreen, a beach towel, and plenty of water to stay hydrated.

2. Embrace Water Sports: The Virgin Islands offer an array of thrilling water sports activities that are perfect for solo travelers. Try your hand at snorkeling, scuba diving, paddleboarding, or kayaking. Many tour operators offer guided excursions, ensuring you have a safe and enjoyable experience exploring the vibrant marine life and stunning coral reefs.

3. Immerse Yourself in Local Culture: Take the opportunity to immerse yourself in the vibrant local culture of the United States Virgin Islands. Visit historic sites such as Blackbeard's Castle in St. Thomas or the Annaberg Sugar Plantation Ruins in St. John. Attend local festivals, taste traditional Caribbean cuisine, and interact with the friendly locals to gain a deeper understanding of the island's rich heritage.

Staying Safe:

1. Inform Others About Your Itinerary: Before embarking on your solo adventure, make sure to inform a trusted friend or family member about your travel plans. Share your itinerary, including the dates and locations of your stay, as well as any activities you plan to participate in. Regularly update them about any changes or unexpected developments during your trip.

2. Stay Vigilant and Aware: While the United States Virgin Islands are generally safe, it's essential to remain vigilant and aware of your surroundings, especially when traveling alone. Avoid walking alone at night in unfamiliar or poorly lit areas, and always trust your instincts. Keep your valuables secure and be cautious of your personal belongings, particularly in crowded tourist areas.

3. Seek Local Advice: Interacting with the locals can provide valuable insights and advice on staying safe while exploring the islands. They are often well-informed about the current safety conditions and can offer recommendations on areas to avoid or precautions to take. Don't hesitate to ask for guidance from hotel staff, tour operators, or trusted locals to ensure a safe and enjoyable experience.

Conclusion:

Traveling solo in the United States Virgin Islands is an incredible opportunity to discover the beauty of this Caribbean destination at your own pace. By following these tips on where to stay, things to do, and how to stay safe, you can make the most of your solo adventure while creating unforgettable memories in this tropical paradise. Remember to embrace the local culture, connect with fellow travelers, and savor every moment of your solo journey in the United States Virgin Islands.

Chapter 42: Tips for Traveling on a Budget in the United States Virgin Islands

Introduction:

Traveling to the United States Virgin Islands (USVI) may seem like an expensive endeavor, but with careful planning and a few budget-friendly tips, you can explore this tropical paradise without breaking the bank. In this chapter, we will provide you with valuable insights on where to stay, things to do, and how to save money during your visit to the USVI.

1. Affordable Accommodation Options:

When it comes to finding budget-friendly accommodations in the USVI, consider staying in guesthouses or vacation rentals instead of high-end resorts. Look for local guesthouses or bed and breakfasts that offer comfortable rooms at affordable rates. Additionally, consider booking accommodations on the less touristy islands like St. Croix, where prices tend to be more reasonable compared to St. Thomas or St. John.

2. Exploring the Natural Beauty:

The USVI is renowned for its stunning beaches, crystal-clear waters, and lush landscapes. Instead of spending money on expensive tours, take advantage of the free and affordable natural attractions available. Visit the pristine Trunk Bay on St. John, which offers free entry and snorkeling opportunities. Hike the beautiful trails of the Virgin Islands National Park, where you can immerse yourself in nature without spending a dime.

3. Local Cuisine:

Eating out can quickly consume your travel budget, but there are ways to enjoy the local cuisine without breaking the bank. Seek out local food trucks or small eateries where you can savor delicious

Caribbean dishes at reasonable prices. Try the local specialty, Roti a flavorful and filling wrap filled with curried meat or vegetables. Additionally, visit local farmers' markets to purchase fresh produce and create your own budget-friendly meals.

4. Affordable Transportation:

Getting around the USVI can be costly, especially if you rely solely on taxis or rental cars. Instead, consider using public transportation options such as buses or shared taxis, known as safari buses. These options are not only cheaper but also provide an opportunity to interact with locals and gain a deeper understanding of the island culture. Additionally, renting a bike or scooter can be a fun and economical way to explore the islands at your own pace.

5. Free Cultural Experiences:

Immerse yourself in the vibrant culture of the USVI without spending a fortune. Attend local festivals, such as the St. John Festival or the Crucian Christmas Festival on St. Croix, where you can enjoy live music, dance performances, and traditional food for free or at a minimal cost. Explore historical sites like Fort Christian in Charlotte Amalie, St. Thomas, which offers free admission and provides fascinating insights into the island's past.

6. Saving on Water Activities:

The USVI is a paradise for water enthusiasts, but water activities can often be expensive. To save money, consider bringing your own snorkeling gear or renting it from local shops instead of joining costly guided tours. Many beaches offer excellent snorkeling opportunities right from the shore. Additionally, look for discounted rates on water sports activities during the off-peak season or negotiate for better prices with local operators.

Conclusion:

Traveling on a budget in the United States Virgin Islands is entirely possible with a little planning and creativity. By opting for affordable accommodations, exploring natural attractions, enjoying local cuisine, utilizing public transportation, participating in free cultural experiences, and saving on water activities, you can make the most of your trip without overspending. Remember, the USVI offers countless breathtaking experiences that won't cost you a fortune, allowing you to create unforgettable memories while staying within your budget.

Chapter 43: Tips for Traveling Responsibly in the United States Virgin Islands

Introduction:

As you embark on your journey to the stunning United States Virgin Islands, it is essential to travel responsibly to ensure the preservation of its pristine environment and rich cultural heritage. By following these tips, you can minimize your impact on the environment and contribute positively to the local communities.

1. Respect the Environment:

The United States Virgin Islands boast breathtaking natural beauty, from crystal-clear waters to lush tropical forests. To minimize your impact on the environment:

- Dispose of waste properly, using designated recycling bins and avoiding littering.

- Conserve water by taking shorter showers and reusing towels.

- Choose eco-friendly activities and tours that promote sustainable practices.

- Avoid touching or disturbing coral reefs and marine life while snorkeling or diving.

2. Support Local Businesses:

By supporting local businesses, you contribute to the economic growth and cultural preservation of the United States Virgin Islands. Here's how you can do it responsibly:

- Shop at local markets and stores to support local artisans and farmers.

- Dine at locally-owned restaurants that serve traditional cuisine made from locally-sourced ingredients.

- Stay at locally-owned accommodations, such as bed and breakfasts or small boutique hotels, to immerse yourself in the local culture.

3. Engage with the Local Community:

To gain a deeper understanding of the United States Virgin Islands' culture and traditions, engage with the local community respectfully:

- Learn about the history and customs of the islands through guided tours or cultural events.

- Respect local customs and traditions, such as appropriate attire when visiting religious sites.

- Engage in responsible volunteering opportunities that positively impact the local community and environment.

4. Preserve Marine Life:

The United States Virgin Islands are renowned for their vibrant marine ecosystems. To protect these fragile habitats and ensure their preservation:

- Choose eco-friendly water activities, such as kayaking or paddleboarding, which have minimal impact on marine life.

- Use reef-safe sunscreen to avoid harmful chemicals that can damage coral reefs.

- Refrain from feeding or touching marine animals, as this can disrupt their natural behavior and habitat.

5. Conserve Energy:

Conserving energy is crucial for reducing your carbon footprint and protecting the environment. Consider the following tips:

- Turn off lights and air conditioning when leaving your accommodation.

- Opt for public transportation, biking, or walking instead of renting a car, when possible.

- Use energy-efficient appliances and turn them off when not in use.

Conclusion:

By traveling responsibly in the United States Virgin Islands, you can contribute to the preservation of its natural wonders and cultural heritage. Remember to respect the environment, support local businesses, engage with the community, preserve marine life, and conserve energy. By doing so, you will leave a positive impact on the islands and ensure their beauty can be enjoyed by future generations.

www.ingramcontent.com/pod-product-compliance
Lightning Source LLC
Chambersburg PA
CBHW021224130726
47988CB00002B/801